stenciling

Ideas & Decorating Techniques

Better Homes and Gardens® Books
Des Moines, Iowa

Better Homes and Gardens® Books
An imprint of Meredith® Books

***Stenciling* Ideas & Decorating Techniques**
Editor: Linda Hallam
Art Director: Jerry J. Rank
Contributing Editors: Susan Andrews, Andrea Caughey, Joetta Moulden
Stencil Design: Tina Blanck, Patricia Mohr Kramer, Amy Queen, Melanie Royal, Wade Scherrer
Photographers: Fran Brennan, Ed Gohlich, Bob Greenspan, Pete Krumhardt
Copy Chief: Catherine Hamrick
Copy and Production Editor: Terri Fredrickson
Book Production Managers: Pam Kvitne, Marjorie J. Schenkelberg
Contributing Copy Editor: Carol Boker
Contributing Proofreaders: Sherry Hames, Susan J. Kling, Willa Speiser
Indexer: Kathleen Poole
Electronic Production Coordinator: Paula Forest
Editorial and Design Assistants: Kaye Chabot, Mary Lee Gavin, Karen Schirm

Meredith® Books
Editor in Chief: James D. Blume
Design Director: Matt Strelecki
Managing Editor: Gregory H. Kayko
Executive Shelter Editor: Denise L. Caringer

Director, Retail Sales and Marketing: Terry Unsworth
Director, Sales, Special Markets: Rita McMullen
Director, Sales, Premiums: Michael A. Peterson
Director, Sales, Retail: Tom Wierzbicki
Director, Sales, Home & Garden Centers: Ray Wolf
Director, Book Marketing: Brad Elmitt
Director, Operations: George A. Susral
Director, Production: Douglas M. Johnston

Vice President, General Manager: Jamie L. Martin

***Better Homes and Gardens®* Magazine**
Editor in Chief: Jean LemMon
Executive Interior Design Editor: Sandra S. Soria

Meredith Publishing Group
President, Publishing Group: Christopher M. Little
Vice President, Consumer Marketing & Interactive Media: Hal Oringer

Meredith Corporation
Chairman and Chief Executive Officer: William T. Kerr

Chairman of the Executive Committee: E. T. Meredith III

Cover Photograph: Bob Greenspan.The room shown is on pages 56-57 and 64-65.

All of us at Better Homes and Gardens® Books are dedicated to providing you with information and ideas to enhance your home. We welcome your comments and suggestions. Write to us at: Better Homes and Gardens® Books, Shelter Editorial Department, 1716 Locust St., Des Moines, IA 50309-3023.

If you would like to purchase any of our books, check wherever quality books are sold.
Visit our website at bhg.com or bhgbooks.com.

First Edition–01
Library of Congress Catalog Card Number: 00-133273
ISBN: 0-696-21115-7

contents

getting started

Imagine drab walls enlivened with trailing vines and blooming flowers, plain floors and ceilings **transformed with rich colors and patterns,** and dated accessories refreshed with lively motifs. **Stenciling and stamping decorating projects** provide you with the tools to do that and more—as well as **help you experience the joy** of artistic expression. Best of all, you don't have to be able to draw or paint to **embellish the surfaces.** With stencils and stamps, you have the freedom to **choose the patterns and colors you love**—whether you decorate your whole house, a room, a wall, or a single piece of furniture.

Look at the **first four chapters for decorating and color inspiration** for every room of your home, including the porch and entry. If you have little ones in your house, note that idea-filled nurseries and children's rooms also are included. **You'll see projects based on** commercial stencils and stamps and on custom patterns, with sources included in this book. **As you plan your projects,** tour the three homes featured in the Home Tour. You'll see how stenciling and stamping **create and define traditional, contemporary, and transitional interiors.** In most rooms featured, one design element—either a stenciled surface or furnishings—stars. In some stunning examples, surfaces, furnishings, and fabrics are all stenciled to give dramatic effect.

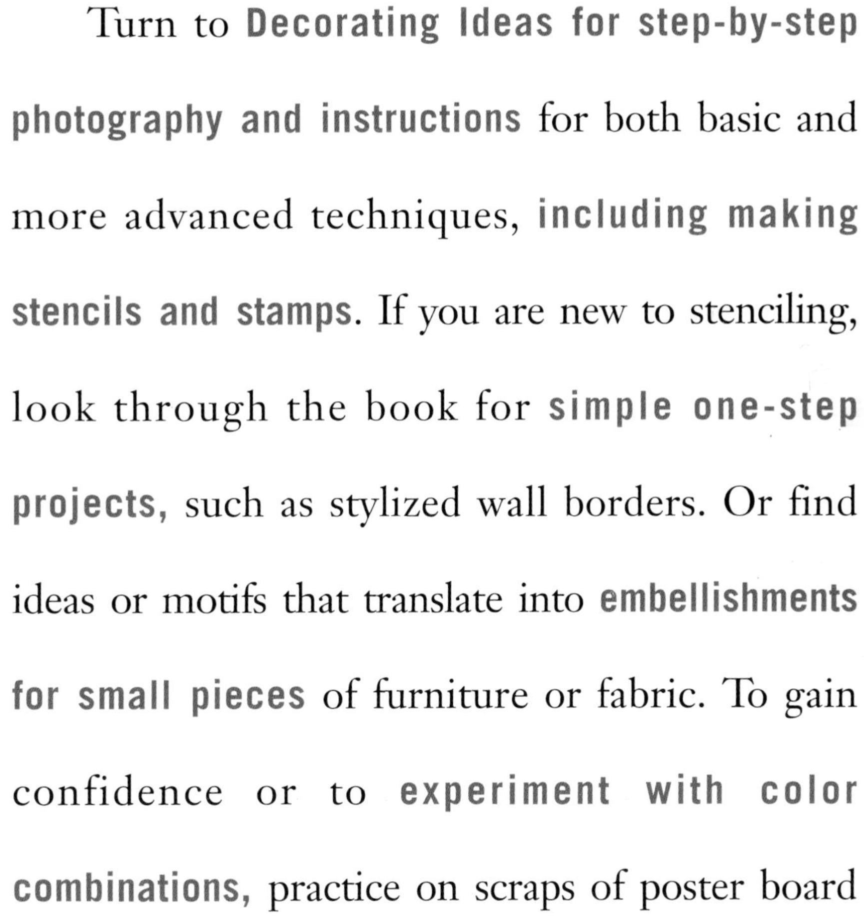

Turn to **Decorating Ideas for step-by-step photography and instructions** for both basic and more advanced techniques, **including making stencils and stamps.** If you are new to stenciling, look through the book for **simple one-step projects,** such as stylized wall borders. Or find ideas or motifs that translate into **embellishments for small pieces** of furniture or fabric. To gain confidence or to **experiment with color combinations,** practice on scraps of poster board until you achieve the look you want. Before beginning a project, **read the tips from skilled stencil artists** on pages 86–87. Their advice will help you choose materials and brushstrokes for pleasing results. Featured projects include materials lists, time and skill estimates, and commercial sources of patterns.

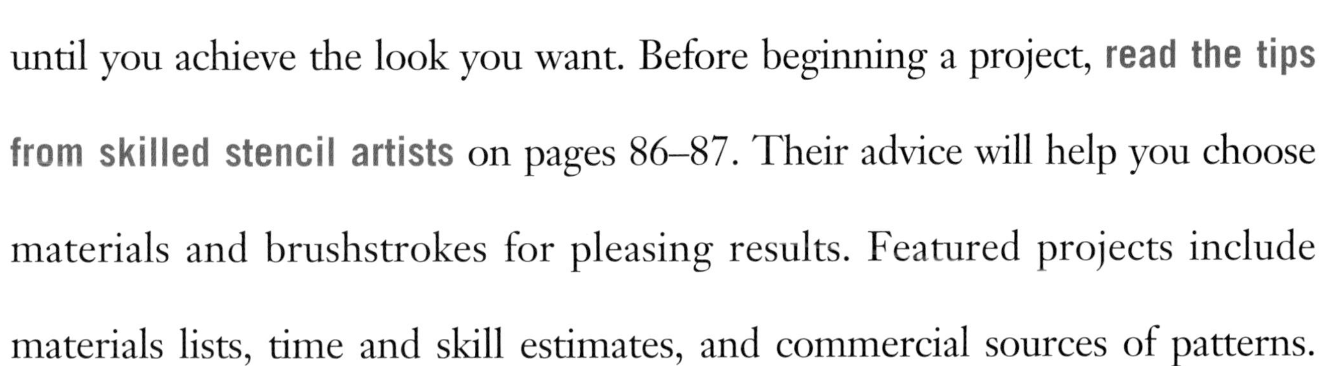

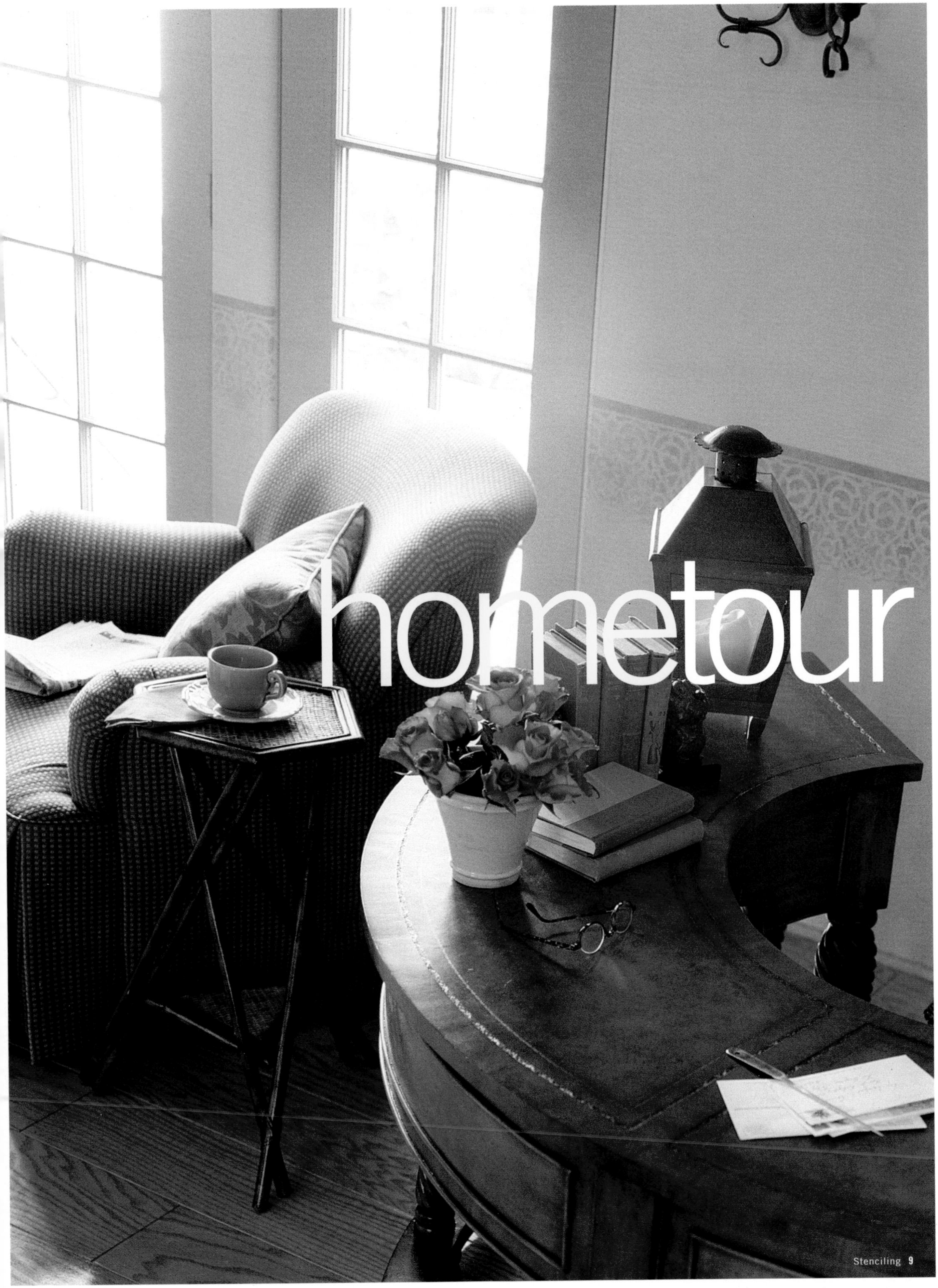

hometour

PersonalizedContemporary

Add your own touches with stenciled accessories based on geometric forms and stylish architectural elements.

WHEN YOUR GOAL IS TO WARM AND DECORATE A WHOLE HOUSE, enhance the instant power of dramatic wall colors with the appeal of stenciling and stamping projects. These economical, do-it-yourself techniques translate to newer, more contemporary houses—and to older cottages and country-style homes. As a beginning, look at the many options for stenciling and stamping. Rather than limiting projects to walls and floors, broaden your decorating by also including stenciled motifs for furnishings, accessories, and fabrics. Look for projects that repeat or enhance architectural elements in your home, such as a motif based on decorative trim or tile. Work with simple motifs, including stenciled or stamped geometric shapes, that translate well into large-scale, eye-catching projects.

Crafted from three hinged doors, the color-block geometric screen, *above,* attests to the strength of the clever placement of simple, large-scale geometric forms. The project features stenciling and reverse stenciling for added design interest. **See page 90 for technique and page 106 for stencil pattern.**

An embossed decorative tile on the firebox surround inspired the stencil motif that dresses up a plain mirror frame, *right.* Two compatible paint colors repeat the color-block idea of the screen, which is placed in the corner across from the mantel. **See page 105 for fireplace mirror frame stencil pattern.**

TOBY TYLER
JAMES OTIS
THE FORBIDDEN TRAIL
THE GREAT LAKES
AMERICA'S BEST-LOVED COMMUNITY RECIPES
PAT CONROY
MAJESTIC

The curved arms of the iron chandelier, *left,* inspire the simple stencil motif for the two borders and the embellished slipcovers. The red wall color sets off the gold tone metallic paint used for the recurring stencil. For a pleasing composition, the upper border aligns slightly below the wall niche, while the lower border is at chair-rail height. The motif repeats on cotton slipcover fabric, which absorbs latex paint. Metallic paint, *below,* transforms a repetitive stencil motif into a decorative border. The rich gold reinforces the sheen of the mirror's double frame to unify the dining room. Gold-tone paint adds sparkle and glamorous touches to elevate the look of furnishings in such areas as dining rooms, which are often used at night and for entertaining. Simple motifs work best when the paint color is the star. **See page 91 for technique and page 105 for stencil pattern.**

A stenciled border based on existing architectural trim decorates the space over the window sink, *above.* Terra-cotta paint warms the open kitchen and provides a rich background for the stenciled border. The white border visually links the painted white cabinets in the carefully edited scheme. This tailored approach works well for a kitchen planned for busy family living and casual entertaining. **See page 88 for technique and page 105 for stencil pattern.**

One stencil can be used two ways as the reverse stencil of the architectural motif border attests, *right.* The reverse stencil technique means that the negative (blank) space of the original stencil becomes the motif. Such a reversal effectively defines separate spaces in a large, open room. The reverse stencil provides a transition between the terra-cotta walls of the kitchen and breakfast area and the stairwell.

The fireplace works as the focal point for the sunny breakfast area, *opposite,* with the addition of the stenciled lattice, enhanced with hand-painted shadows. The backdrop introduces a charming garden ambience appropriate to the woven chairs and skirted table. Accessories, such as the grapevine wreath and topiaries, can be changed to reflect the season or occasion. **See page 112 for stencil sources.**

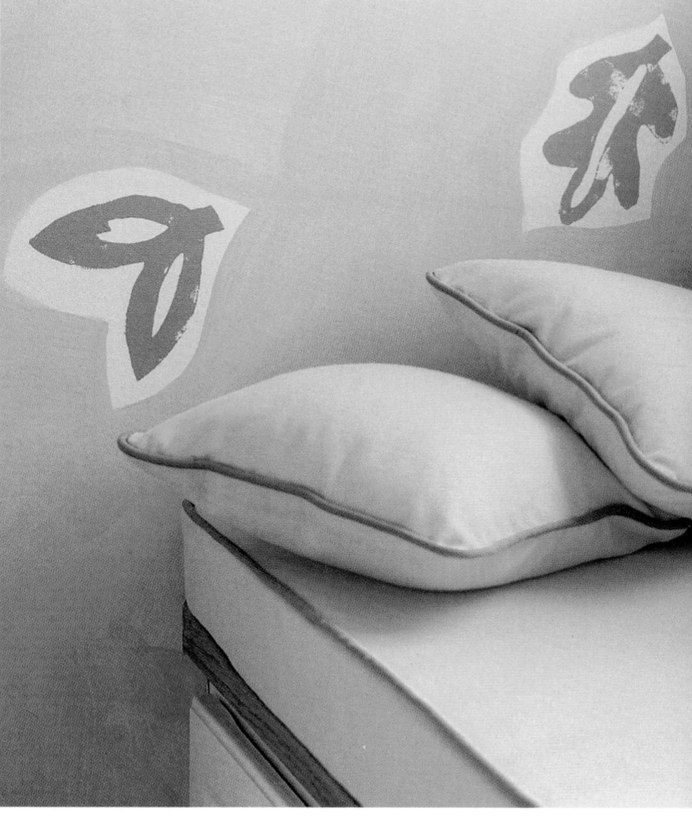

The wonderfully bright duvet and sham, with motifs designed to emulate hand-painted fabric, set the style and color scheme for this teenage girl's room, *opposite.* Bright pink and blue leaves, positioned as though they are drifting from a tree, are casually stamped on the white wall. After the leaves were outlined, a brushed-on coat of bright green glaze energizes the scheme with upbeat, youthful color. The white iron bed contributes an interesting shape, and the open design allows the wall to stand out. As an alternative, a wooden bed or pair of twin beds could be painted crisp white or snappy colors that complement the decorating scheme.

Graphic shapes echo the motifs and colors of the stamped bedroom walls. The pink tulip lamp on the yellow-skirted table, *above left,* recalls the popular "flower power" look of the 1960s, in vogue again. With vibrant, playful walls and fabrics, a minimum of accessories works best. No wall art is needed as the stamped walls become the engaging art. For another decorating option, one wall could be stamped and the other three glazed in the green.

With colorful stamped and glazed walls as the focal point, other design elements, such as the piped seat cushion and accent pillows, *above right,* naturally play off the scheme. The stamped walls and duvet fabric provide lively pattern while the solid cotton duck pillows balance with visual relief that doesn't distract. The blue piping repeats the blue in the duvet fabric and stamped leaves. **See page 92 for technique and page 105 for stencil patterns.**

Fashionable imported sheer fabric with appliquéd flowers and vines combined with a pretty shade of periwinkle blue inspire this bedroom designed for a teenage girl, *opposite.* The cool shade plus the crisp white illustrate the strong design and youthful sophistication of a carefully edited scheme. Stenciled white flowers and vines embellish periwinkle walls, while periwinkle flowers enliven white fabrics. White flowers on sheer fabric cover periwinkle accent pillows. The white feather-boa-style lamp and white accent pillows add the finishing feminine touches to the pretty scheme.

Plain surfaces, such as the window treatment cornice, *top left,* provide balance in rooms decorated with stenciled motifs. When an eye-catching border receives the attention, plain surfaces provide the necessary balance. For impact at ceiling height, the border flower size is enlarged from the fabric.

Stenciled flowers and vines from the same pattern transform plain white cotton fabric into a beautifully detailed duvet cover and oversize pillow sham, *left.* To exactly match the walls, the same periwinkle latex paint is used for the stenciled flowers. For polished decorating touches, pillows wrapped in the sheer fabric are detailed with tailored piping, and the larger accent pillow sports a ruffled trim. **See page 93 for technique and page 106 for stencil patterns.**

Enriching the **Ranch**

Turn to the power of detailed stenciling to transform plain walls and collected furniture into politely polished, traditional rooms.

CONSIDER BASIC ROOMS WITH NO ARCHITECTURAL DETAILING as blank canvases that allow you to experiment with your favorite styles, motifs, and colors. Use paint and stenciling projects as the tools to create the rooms of your dreams. For the prettiest rooms, plan which ones will spotlight stenciled surfaces and which will feature decorated furniture and accessories. When walls are the focal point, use plain furniture for balance. Or, for a lively twist, as illustrated in the living room of this ranch-style house, opt for neutral colors for plain walls and flooring and allow stenciled furniture and accessories to be the center of attention. Small surfaces, such as tabletops, work well as palettes to experiment with more detailed, ornate stencil patterns and techniques.

● Rosy-beige glazed walls, painted brick, and a Berber area rug team up as a backdrop for painted tables, a slipcovered sofa, and vintage accessories, *opposite.* The pairing of blues and greens—from the painted table base to stenciled details to the blue fabric—relaxes the traditional mood. Touches of paint highlight details on the turned legs of the drop-leaf table.

● Stenciling hides the faults of time-worn pieces, such as the drop-leaf table, *below.* To mask minor damage, the tabletop was

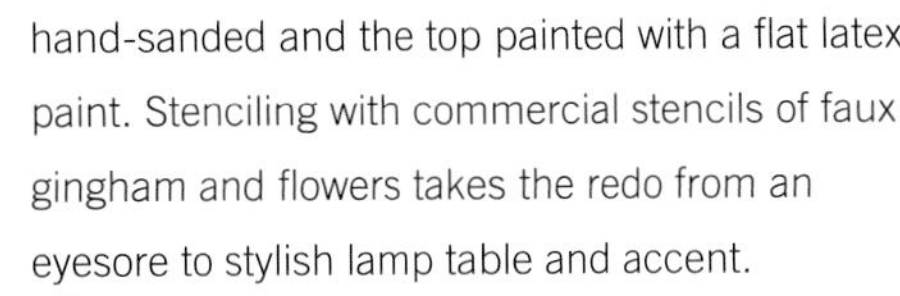

hand-sanded and the top painted with a flat latex paint. Stenciling with commercial stencils of faux gingham and flowers takes the redo from an eyesore to stylish lamp table and accent.

● Unfinished pieces such as this coffee table, *above,* provide ideal surfaces to decorate. Mustard yellow paint warms the background for the stenciled vines. A final coat of an antiquing glaze ages the effect. **See page 112 for stencil sources.**

For a stylized interpretation of a traditional floral spray, the motifs stenciled over the sliding glass doors, *above,* include five floral elements. The garden mix, artfully arranged by the stencil artist, features hydrangea, roses, irises, morning glories, and twigs. Soft colors reflect the mood and timeless appeal of an English flower garden in early summer.

A decorative screen, *below,* enlivens the formal dining room by repeating the floral theme of the stenciled spray. The arched tops repeat the curves of the iron chandelier to introduce a pleasing repetition. For a light, airy touch, only one flower, the poppy, is stenciled over the stylized, pale green background.

Carefully chosen decorative elements change the plain dining room, with sliding patio doors, into a pretty, traditional setting, *above.* To keep the room light and airy, free-form stenciled floral motifs, positioned by the artist and connected by freehand strokes, substitute for a window top treatment. A neatly stenciled

screen, crafted from pressed particleboard and joined with piano hinges, animates a blank corner. In the garden style of the dining room, the screen features an airy overall design, highlighted with a sprinkling of flowers and leaves. Enhancing the effect, a stained glass panel transforms an oddly placed window into a design element. The candle-style chandelier illuminates the table and Queen-Anne-style chairs. A wire plant stand, brimming with blooming hydrangea, takes advantage of the the sunny setting, while a smaller stand with a topiary strengthens the garden room ambience. **See page 112 for stencil sources.**

A traditional floral fabric with a deep scarlet background, *opposite,* provides the starting point for the traditional decorating scheme of a dine-in kitchen. To enrich a once-drab space, scarlet red paint stylishly updates stained cabinets. The stenciled border, with a grapevine motif replicating the colorful print drapery fabric, repeats the border in the breakfast area. Stenciled, carefully detailed grapes, roses, and ivy soften the stylized effect. Accessories, such as the metal tole tray, reflect the inviting updated cottage style.

Different values of the same medium blue paint add dimension to the series of scrolls, formed into a cartouche stenciled on the painted tabletop, *below.* The stencil pattern duplicates motifs of classic transferware, such as the early-19th-century bowl shown here.

Blue-and-white porcelain and pottery and a love of the garden inspire the cheerful and charming breakfast area, *above.* Painted and stenciled furniture pairs with a grapevine trellis border for a lightly decorated room. The glazed rosy beige backdrop with a hint of terra-cotta recalls aged garden walls. The stenciled grapevine trellis frames the cupboard with the addition of the gracefully draped grapes and ivy. A trio of wall-hung platters neatly fits the space between the cupboard and border; the open shelves display prized collectibles. Painted a soft white to match the cupboard, the round table is stenciled in a scroll motif while the seats of the traditional chairs are upholstered in a fresh, stylish, blue-and-yellow toile. **See page 112 for stencil sources.**

This home office and guest room combination, *right,* takes on an exotic air with dark woods and Asian touches. The mood recalls richly appointed and highly detailed late-19th-century interiors. The damask motif, in the style of the fabric, creates an overall wall pattern that unifies the disparate elements into an inviting scheme. The stenciled gold-toned border details the face of the crown molding. An ornately framed mirror reflects the scene.

The stenciled damask pattern, *below,* contributes the illusion of texture to the arrangement of the one-of-a-kind custom lamp, beautifully detailed tole tray, and antique teapot used as a vase for daffodils. **See page 95 for technique and page 112 for stencil sources.**

A double closet is converted into the computer work space of the home office, *above*. To embellish the space, the wall and shelves are painted a deep teal and stenciled in gold paint with a tile motif. Stenciled tiles frame a tole tray.

Enlarged tile patterns, reminiscent of those stenciled above the desk, decorate purchased velvet pillows, *right*. Metallic paints continue the rich, exotic touches that recall both the Far East and Renaissance

paintings. The combination of pillows in an array of colors, shapes, sizes, and trims turns a reproduction metal daybed into a luxurious cocoon for reading.

A vintage hanging fixture, *left,* makes a dramatic design statement, enhanced by the stenciled medallion. The effect recalls the medallions that graced the ceilings of Victorian homes. Similar medallion patterns are stenciled in the four corners of the home office and a midsection of the crown molding to add visual interest and pattern.

Decorative motifs turn utilitarian surfaces into art-inspired fine furniture. For an opulent mix of patterns and textures, this plywood desk surface, *lower left,* is stenciled in brown over a gold-tone background. The teal and gold border repeats the combination that highlights the crown molding. These patterns and luminous colors recall the jewel-tone fabrics featured in Italian Renaissance paintings.

See page 112 for stencil sources.

An old oak dresser takes on a lighter, more sophisticated air with a lightly distressed white paint finish, *right.* To echo the mirror, the curved drawer fronts are stenciled with a shell design, that traditionally has been carved into furniture. A white shade on the candlestick-style lamp and silver accessories complete the charming arrangement.

Echoing the delicate wall stencils, a discreet ribbon trellis in two soft shades decorates the top of a painted chest, *below.* This minimal color sets a chic, yet romantic mood for a bedroom. Furniture can be sealed with a matte-finish polyurethane to prevent chipping and undue wear.

Delicately glazed and stenciled walls create a springtime background for an old iron bed and oak dresser, both freshened with white paint, *opposite.* In the essence of a garden arbor, the background stencil depicts a ribbon trellis, while green glaze softens the effect. The trellis pattern comes to life with an overlay of a stenciled wisteria vine in full bloom. The vine cascades in subtle detailing between the iron bed and the painted dresser. This garden wall scene turns a small bedroom into a pretty, serene setting. The coverlet and sham in a delicate wisteria print enhance the airy garden mood. The plaid accent pillow, piped in a fresh green, repeats the lavender and green of the two-color palette and contributes a pleasing round shape. The quilt emphasizes the old-fashioned garden theme without the distraction of additional color or pattern. **See page 112 for stencil sources.**

ck

An ornate mirror frame, *opposite,* sets the scene for the makeover of a once-ordinary small bath. For the new chic look, an overall damask pattern stencil repeats the pattern of the carved mirror. Two shades of purple glaze are combed over a pearlescent base coat. The cultured-marble counter and backsplash, primed and painted with a platinum shade, finish the bath decorating in chic style. Sconce lighting illuminates the sink.

Paint and stencils create the look of embossed metal for the decorative cabinet doors, *right.* For this sophisticated effect, old painted doors are first sanded and primed. A stencil treatment, based on a textural paste, adds dimension to the center of each cabinet door. For the appearance of burnished metal, black latex paint, simply brushed on, deepens the effect. Silver metallic paint is applied over the black base coat and sanded lightly on the top edges of the relief to reveal the black. Antique glass cabinetry pulls complete the transformation from drab to dramatic. **See page 94 for technique and page 112 for stencil sources.**

Spanish-style **Rambler**

A chair-rail border, created from glaze and subtle stencil motifs, dresses up the open living spaces of a remodeled California ranch.

CONSIDER STENCILED CHAIR RAILS or other similarly subdued techniques to impart architectural interest to plain living or dining areas. As a first step, choose a design motif compatible with both the style of your home and your decorating taste. Look at existing features, such as a decorative fireplace surround or the pattern in a fabric or rug, for inspiration. For an interesting backdrop that does not overpower, choose a simplified design that blends with your wall color. Study the placement of windows, doors, and other openings to determine the most pleasing height. For an easier alternative, stencil the chair rail directly below your windows.

A major remodeling transformed a standard ranch-style home with hints of gracious Spanish Colonial style. The stenciled chair-rail border, *right,* adds interesting detailing to the open living room and calls attention to the arched doorway and narrow casement windows. The arch frames a view into the dining room, detailed with the same mosaic-style stencil. Neutral colors animate the open spaces without competing with the handsomely detailed sconces and sophisticated furnishings. **See page 112 for stencil sources.**

In the subtle technique, *right,* the wall area used as a chair rail is glazed and stenciled. The border aligns with muntins of the French windows for a neat appearance. Warm shades of tan balance the plank floor and provide a soothing background for a collection of antique and reproduction furniture, including the gently curved desk and European-style armchair. Accessories, such as the antique lantern and old books, enhance the sophisticated, yet muted, wall detailing.

Gentle arches frame the views from room to room in the open plan, *left.* The sophisticated glazed and stenciled chair rail enlivens the living room and adjoining dining room without distracting from the arches and narrow French windows—both key elements of the Spanish Colonial style. Sofas face each other in the center of the room, allowing the chair rail to be the backdrop for a cupboard display and a pair of flanking chairs. Walls showcase collected contemporary art.

Soft, earthy colors and a raised tiled hearth, *opposite,* impart a sense of the patio garden to the recessed fireplace. The stenciled chair rail wraps the opening of the arch, cleverly detailing the space. The burnt bamboo plant stand gives a strong silhouette against the stenciling, while the patterned rug adds a complementary pattern for design interest. The curved detailing of the iron sconce recalls the stencil's exotic curves. **See page 112 for stencil sources.**

The stenciled ceiling medallion repeats and balances the motifs of the chair-rail border, *opposite,* in the formal dining room. To enrich the Spanish Colonial flavor, bullnose edges replace window casings. The bamboo shade controls light and views without the intrusion of fussy treatments. The monochromatic color scheme replicates the sophisticated palette seen throughout the house. Scrollwork—from the stenciled border to the cast table base to the carved detailing of the chairs—unifies the room. Overscaled pieces, such as the scrolled table base and sideboard, give substance to the setting. The leaning mirror, with egg-and-dart molding, imparts a sophisticated backdrop to the print and obelisk.

The stenciled and glazed medallion, *left,* recalls the traditional, ornate plaster medallions of grand 18th- and 19th-century homes. The shape repeats the curves of the reproduction metal and glass-globe chandelier. The placement of the motifs to decorative points and the mosaic effects allude to the exotic Moorish influences that appear in 1920s interpretations of Spanish-style houses. Frosted globes direct light to the ceiling medallion. **See page 112 for stencil sources.**

living&dining

living&dining

From mid-20th-century retro cool to flowery cottage charm, stenciled motifs create rooms to fit any decorating mood.

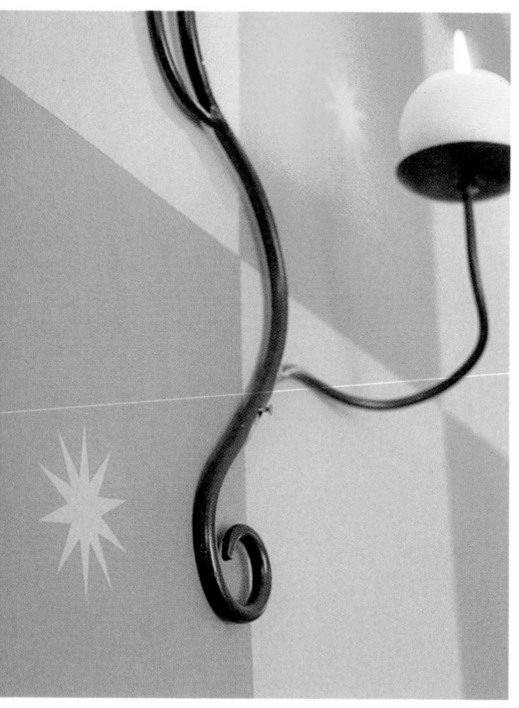

JAZZY SUBURBAN. Transform a chimney breast or plain wall into a design focal point with an energetic, painted checkerboard pattern. Tape off and paint the background as a two-color grid. Stencil the motif in the lighter color inside the darker rectangles. Instead of art, simplify with contemporary sconces and sleek glass accessories.

The checkerboard grid with stylized stars, *left,* freshens an inviting living room devoted to fashionable and fun mid-20th-century design.

Paint and stenciled stars lighten and brighten a living room, *right,* once dominated by dark oak woodwork and a dreary brick fireplace. Minimal accessories—sconces and vases—allow the checkerboard and furnishings to shine. The sun-porch bar offers another take on spirited stencil and stamped designs. **See page 98 for technique and page 112 for stencil sources.**

LOUIS ART FAIR

JAZZY SUBURBAN. If you enjoy entertaining at home and have a designated space for a bar, consider the possibilities of theme decorating. Although the patterns are included for the stenciled martini glass and stamped olives shown here, other motifs—such as wine glasses or champagne flutes—would be equally fun. For a breakfast area, stencil coffee mugs or tea cups and saucers. When you repeat one motif, skew it at various angles for interesting effects. **See page 93 for additional directions on making custom stencils or consult stencil sources listed on page 112 for commercial stencils.**

Careful planning translates into harmonious design when two adjacent rooms, *below left,* feature stenciled walls. The living room in the foreground includes a checkerboard focal point. The remaining living room walls are painted, not stenciled. The cased opening frames the view into the bar, where walls are stenciled and stamped from floor-to-ceiling with martini glasses and olives.

The classic martini glass, with a pimiento-stuffed olive, *below right,* tilts as part of its casual charm. The hand-drawn look of the stenciled glass recalls the 1950s—the heyday of advertising art.

With martini glasses as the backdrop, *opposite,* a vintage bar and barstools set the scene for convivial gatherings. Bamboo shades and the hanging pendant are popular mid-20th-century icons. Barware, including the martini shaker, adds the final touch. **See page 98 for technique and page 107 for patterns.**

Better Homes and Gardens
GARDEN
STYLE

GARDENER'S COTTAGE. Choose a fabric you love as the inspiration for a personal decorating scheme. Look for a pattern with both the colors for the background walls and furniture and the motifs to translate into stencils. Graphic, stylized motifs are ideal because stenciled details can be simplified. Depending on your time and skill, base one or several stencils on the fabric.

The youthful floral print, *opposite,* works perfectly as the design inspiration for a living room decorated in the garden cottage style. The fabric's grid design repeats in a larger scale for the painted wall, created with masking tape and two colors of paint. Five motifs are pulled from the fabric to create the stencils, with designs randomly stenciled. Purchased unfinished, a painted armoire anchors a corner and displays plants settled in baskets. Accent pillows in compatible fabrics finish the look in style.

The white background allows stenciled flowers in botanical motifs to appear as though they are framed, *above.* Subtle shading and delicate green leaves combine as naturalistic interpretation without the necessity of detailed overlays. **See page 93 for directions for making custom stencils.**

GARDENER'S COTTAGE. Think beyond the obvious when you decorate with stenciled motifs. Rather than limiting yourself to conventional borders or overall patterns, consider other interesting applications. To work in the garden style, look at ways to gracefully incorporate flowers and vines into the decorating scheme. Use fresh colors—such as pale, sunny yellow, light green, and blue—and delicate motifs to capture the essence of garden cottages. The simplest detailing and the lightest touch are appropriate to this appealing, youthful look.

A restrained yellow-and-white palette, chosen for the pretty living room, *opposite,* recalls the charm of sunny garden cottages. Classic combinations are easy to create and impart a lighthearted quality to a room. For extra detailing and an alternative to a conventionally placed border, a combination of hand painting and stenciling frames the whitewashed paneled door. To create this whimsical look, the border is hand-drawn with yellow pencil to match the wall color, then washed with a white paint and glaze combination. A delicate, stylized vine border, based on the slipcover fabric, is stenciled in shades of blue and green. To complete the charming setting, white paint refreshes small tables from a secondhand store. The tables are painted, rather than decorated, to allow the border to receive the most attention in the setting. Plants and books complete the youthful and appealing look.

Lively, happy colors infuse the wall and border with the feeling of springtime even on the coldest winter days.The wash of a white-tinted glaze over the yellow, *left,* allows the base coat to subtly show through for a hint of color. Two shades of green and a periwinkle blue add cooler colors of nature to the setting. Soft curves, rather than straight lines, recall meandering garden paths and country streams.

VAN GOGH
Women, Art, and Society
OLD WOMAN
country garden planner
garden style projects
SINGER SARGENT
MOTHER & CHILD in Art
HISTLER A RETROSPECTIVE

GARDENER'S COTTAGE. Open your dining area to sunshine with a color palette and decorating scheme based on the outdoors. For a youthful look, balance shades of sky blue with sunny yellow and crisp white. Update woodwork and furnishings with white paint as an instant way to lighten and brighten. To keep the decorating charmingly modest, stencil detailing rather than overall effects. (Busy overall stenciled walls can visually close in a small room.) Choose uncomplicated white accessories for this pared-down look.

Designed from the printed shade fabric, the stylized stenciled floral border accents glazed walls, *left*. The border's pale glazed background showcases the delicate blooming vine. The painted plate rack above the border repeats the horizontal line of the border and adds secure display for plates and mugs. The symmetry of the white rack and plates visually balances the white furniture below. The dining tabletop and chair seats introduce natural wood into the pale scheme. An unfinished chest, painted with durable white enamel to match, provides additional convenient storage.

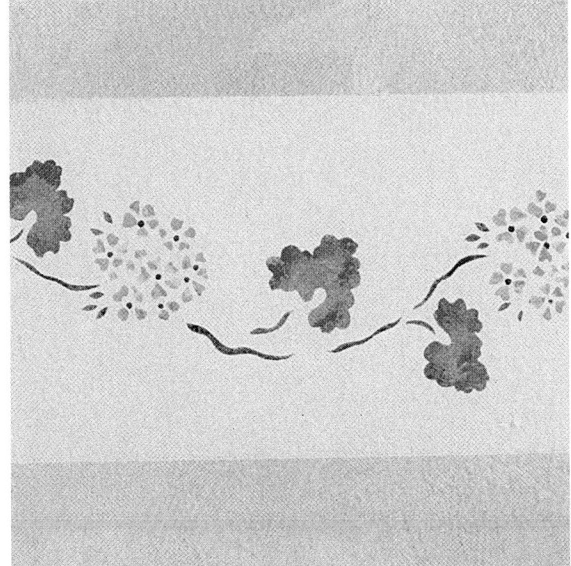

Inspired by an imported sheer fabric with appliquéd white butterflies, a stenciled vine artfully tops the window, *above*. The white drapery rod and standard clips complement without distracting from the springtime butterflies and blooming vines theme. As the stenciled vines accent, the motifs introduce variety without overpowering the pale walls.

The lightly glazed blue wall creates an appealing background for the stenciled border, *left*. White over blue contributes a crisp touch that allows the flowers to shine, while the delicate stenciled motif resembles hand painting. **See page 112 for stencil sources.**

COUNTRY IN THE CITY. When country decorating is your joy, personalize your rooms with the charm of stenciled borders. Since colonial days, stenciled patterns have been prized as economical tools that decorate and add color to rooms. For a fresh, clean version of country-style, combine garden motifs and spring green and sunny yellow fabrics with traditional country furniture and accessories. The combination is charming and easy to emulate.

The botanical slipcover fabric, *upper left,* sets the decorating scheme in this country-style parlor. Rather than replicate the fabric's leaf motif, a compatible ginkgo leaf from a commercial stencil graces the light green walls. A vintage secondhand mirror, its distressed frame untouched, reflects the scene.

The meandering vine appears to grow around the plain oak woodwork, *lower left.* The whimsical effect updates the somewhat serious carved settee, an early-20th-century piece.

Detailed by the stenciled gingko leaves, *opposite,* the cased opening captures a view into the adjacent dining room. As a compatible and not competing technique to stenciling, decoratively painted moiré stripes update the furnishings in the dining room. In the living room, an antique grandfather clock and artwork stand out against the stenciled wall. **See page 99 for technique and page 112 for stencil sources.**

To emphasize a collection of antique olive oil jars, *left,* the deep green stenciled border recalls the classical leaf motifs of Greece and Italy. The dark green gives weight and impact to the stenciled border and balances the deep tones of the jars. A pale color of the stencil would have seemed visually unbalanced.

A deep shade of pumpkin instantly energizes the dining room, *below.* Blackish green paint enriches the crown molding above the stylized border. The placement of the border slightly below the molding makes the ceiling appear higher. A simple, frameless mirror, scenic print, and metal serving stand are unified by the backdrop. **See page 112 for stencil sources.**

BORDER BY DESIGN. For a sophisticated accent, consider a tailored border compatible with the style and furnishings of your room. Position a stenciled border in a living or dining room as you would a wallpaper border—taking into account the background color of the wall as well as art and accessories as you determine the border motif. Deep rich walls, as well as light pale walls, are equally suitable for stenciled borders. The key to choosing interesting paint colors is to ensure sufficient contrast between the border and backdrop. If you decorate an older or a historic-style home, browse through architectural history or period decorating books for stencil pattern ideas. Or consult the listed stencil sources, see page 112, for appropriate and tasteful reproductions of period stencils.

In an early-20th-century house, the natural simplicity of the stylized leaf-and-berry border, *opposite,* complements the Arts and Crafts style of a sitting area enriched with paneled wainscoting. The background warms the setting and lightens the effect of the oak French doors while the stencil introduces pattern and color. **See page 112 for stencil sources.**

bed&bath

bed&bath

Unleash your imagination and decorate to suit your fancy. With stencil motifs, projects range from subtle to sensational.

WOVEN WITH PAINT. Choose neutral colors, such as warm shades of tan and off-white, and tailored stencil patterns for a serene master bedroom. For a shared room, aim for a relaxed look with calm colors and patterns. Turn to paint and stenciled motifs to upgrade features, such as a wall of closets.

Once-drab closet doors, *right,* contribute soft color and the illusion of texture to this master bedroom. The basket-weave stencil creates an overall pattern that warms without dominating the room. The pattern repeats in a pair of accent pillows, stenciled with fabric paint to unify the scheme. Touches of deep red in the fabric-covered headboard and the floral accent pillows introduce necessary lively color. Light wood and wicker accessories finish in natural style.

See page 112 for stencil sources.

TULIP TIME. Refresh a bedroom with a floral theme translated from fashionable appliquéd sheer fabric. The springtime look adapts well for a young girl's room, as shown—or with different furnishings and accessories for a romantic adult bedroom. Start with hand-painted stripes, in cool blue and green, as a tailored background for tulips that are created with commercial stencils. With the popularity of sheer fabrics and ready-made sheer drapery panels, it's easy to find flowers and motifs to set your theme.

Paired with stripes, stenciled tulips update a small upstairs bedroom, *left.* Tulips repeat on the painted and stenciled, scalloped edge floorcloth to neatly unify the decorating scheme. The balance of white, from the narrow stripes and ceiling to the furniture, brightens and visually expands the room. White paint also works magic in updating a dark spindle bed to work with traditional white wicker. A new chenille bedspread, woven in classic style, and crisp linens dress the bed.

A light pouncing motion gives stenciled tulips a charming hand-painted look, *above left,* in the style of botanical art. The commercial stencil features softer lines and more detailing than the appliqué tulip and is compatible with the folk art look. The two-color scheme with blue tulips transforms a traditional motif into a stylish setting.

Floorcloth fabric cut into an oval scalloped rug provides a smooth, sturdy surface for a painted background and stenciled tulips, *above right.* Repeating the color scheme of the striped walls, two tulip motifs are stenciled inside the painted border to add appealing decorative interest. A polyurethane sealer on the floorcloth ensures long wear and continued beauty. **See page 97 for technique and page 112 for stencil sources.**

EASY LEAVES. Decorate a bath quickly and economically with stylish double-stamped leaves. Use this easy technique as an alternative to wallpaper for detailing all four walls or as an accent wall in a bath or powder room. For a garden-fresh look, start with a fresh coat of light paint, such as pale yellow. To ensure a soft natural look, choose soft shades of green and yellow for the leaves. Restrict accessories to white and natural tones for a nature-oriented theme. As an alternative, work in the rich colors of fall foliage with an earthy terra-cotta or taupe for the background and rich reds and browns for the stamped leaves.

The casual placement of the leaves to emulate gently blowing breezes, *above,* heightens the charm and style of stamping. Leaves are in a blending, yet contrasting, shade so that they are clearly visible. Uncomplicated double stamping—a yellow tint stamped over previously stamped green leaves—softens for a serene, natural look.

A small powder room comes to life with paint and artfully stamped cascading leaves, *opposite.* For the freshest, most current look, a pale background color, such as a tint of yellow, apple green, or lavender, visually expands the small space. Leaves are stamped randomly without measuring or spacing. If too many leaves are stamped and the effect appears crowded, paint out excess leaves before stamping the second coat of paint. A white fabric shade, white mirror frame and shelf, and stacked white towels finish in clean spa-style. Accessories are limited to white cups and a forsythia-filled glass.

BUNNY IN THE GARDEN. When you love the garden, bring in the outdoors for your baby or toddler. With a combination of hand painting and stenciling, you can create a cheerful room that will be fun and stimulating throughout the preschool years.

The garden nursery, *opposite,* owes its charm to the overscaled flowers and the soft painterly effects achieved by glaze and sea sponges. For the picket fence, self-adhesive paper, drawn and cut as pickets, covers the original white walls. When the self-adhesive paper is removed, the charming fence remains. The hand-painted bird and birdhouse personalize the scene.

Vegetable stencils and hand-painted details animate the painted chest, *above left,* for a distinctive furniture piece. The drapery tieback, cut from plywood and painted, adds a jaunty touch. Even a butterfly gets into the act in a stenciled motif.

The hand-painted bunny, *above right,* leaps over stenciled vegetables as a wall detail. The freehand painting and detailing soften the stenciled effect and imbue the room with whimsical, folk art charm. The stenciled pillow decorates a vintage rocker that has been freshened with crisp white paint.

A neatly stenciled ladybug lights on a stylized flower, *left*—just one of the charming, lighthearted details in this room.

See page 102 for technique and page 110 for patterns.

PLAYFUL PETS. Unleash your creativity and energize a nursery or toddler's room with primary colors translated into a cheerful dog-and-cat theme. Start with lively, hand-painted stripes as a whimsical background for the fun of framed pet portraits and framed icons of the pet world. Make sure the playful mood continues by extending the theme with painted and stenciled furniture, themed pillows, and window treatments detailed with stenciled dog bones.

Brimming with energy, the engaging nursery, *above,* combines bright colors and strong graphic shapes into an appealing theme. The basic shapes and stylized motifs, in crayon colors, recall the storybooks beloved by generations of young children. To keep the action rolling, the striped wall and shade pair with the painted plaid top of the stenciled toy

chest. Repetition of bright colors unifies the scheme. Vibrant bright red accents transform the window casings and frames into focal points. While the classic white bed gives relief in the colorful milieu, the tailored bumper pad and mattress cover feature the combination of acid green and dark blue. A fashion-conscious baby or curious toddler will be quite at home in such a stylish and visually stimulating setting.

● A vintage wicker chair, *above,* joins the show with the addition of a red-and-white check cushion and green pillow embellished with stenciled bones. Bones also grace the top of the window cornice, finished neatly with a scalloped edge and fabric-covered red buttons. **See page 102 for technique and page 109 for stencil patterns.**

OLD-FASHIONED FLOWER GARDEN. Savor the charm of country gardens and cottage-style decorating with a bedroom detailed with one commercial floral stencil used two ways. By choosing a free-form stencil that can be turned to fit different spaces, you can achieve a graceful effect without dominating the look. The secret is to use a soft background color and widely space the stencil for an airy background.

The glazed wall creates a soothing background for the stenciled headboard, *above.* The white background of the simple, curved wooden headboard contrasts with the blue wall for fresh decorative interest. The crisply tailored yellow-and-white check pillow shams add youthful, country-fresh accents.

Planned as a nursery nook for a new baby, *opposite,* the under-the-eaves space of a master bedroom features a delicately stenciled floral wall as a pretty focal point. Background walls are glazed a light turquoise. The free-form floral stencil includes vines and greenery for an open, airy quality. The stencil is turned as it is positioned for gentle curves and natural detailing. The deep purplish blue of the larger flowers visually anchors the motifs, while yellow touches and tiny pink blooms add lively accents. For tailored contrast, privacy, and sun control, a green-and-white cotton plaid fabric covers the window.

See page 112 for stencil sources.

MAD FOR MOSAICS. Turn to the power of color and the versatility of stencil patterns to update a tired bath. Choose a color scheme that allows the stenciled motif to shine and add accessories and finishing touches that contribute colorful, stylish accents.

Color, as the background and in the stenciled mosaic-style border, *opposite,* solves the decorating dilemma of a bath with a pink sink and green tile walls. In lieu of the costly and time-consuming project of retiling walls and changing the sink, the stenciled mosaic shifts the focus to the walls. Purple pairs with green as the eye-catching, stylized mosaic pattern stenciled over sunny yellow walls. The vertical mosaic, bordering a window, visually heightens the space for more gracious proportions. The vintage etched cabinet mirror and the sconces neatly fit the updated setting.

The commercial stencil pattern includes a corner medallion, *above left,* necessary for a smooth transition from horizontal to vertical borders. Purple and yellow towels repeat the paint colors and add jolts of vibrant color above the medium and light green tiles.

Repetition of motifs unifies a decorating theme. The pegboard towel rack echoes the wave motif of the stylized stenciled mosaic border, *above right.* The mosaic wave reinterprets a classical pattern into a contemporary theme, created with a stock commercial stencil. The pegboard rack from a home furnishings store replicates the shapes while adding dimension and the convenience of additional pegs. **See page 103 for technique and page 112 for stencil sources.**

MONKEYS ON PATROL. Let your imagination run wild and design a room targeted to your child's interests and loves. If your son or daughter has a favorite animal, such as the mischievous monkey featured here, you've found a fun starting point. Look for a commercial stencil or stencils in your theme—or find a fabric that can be simplified for a custom stencil. Work with colors appropriate for the animal and its background so your young naturalist can feel part of the habitat.

Warm, natural colors are an appropriate setting for the monkey and the jungle of this boy's room, *right.* A jungle-theme-printed fabric translates into duvet covers for the bunk beds. Natural bamboo blinds contribute an appropriate window treatment while guaranteeing privacy and sun control. Wall-mounted baskets neatly corral playful monkeys and other stuffed animals, while a larger wicker basket serves as a perfect toy hamper. The dark red desk and bookcase and green chair repeat colors from the stenciled red balls and the foliage.

Although he frolics in a jungle setting, this fun-loving monkey with a red ball in each paw, *above,* obviously has visited the circus. Stenciled details, added as an overlay, create his quizzical expression. To further replicate the jungle theme, palm fronds are cut from sponges and stamped on the hand-painted vines. Two shades of green paint, some lightly stamped, enhance the natural appearance of the fronds. **See pages 100–101 for technique and pages 107–108 for patterns.**

special places

specialplaces

Beautifully detailed stenciled motifs enrich an entry hall for a gracious welcome and preview of the stylish rooms that follow.

HANDSOME HALLWAY. Create an inviting first impression by choosing stencil motifs that enrich your entry hall. Select patterns and colors that enhance architectural elements and set the stage for your decorating scheme.

● A banded stencil border, *left,* adds depth to the ceiling, while the more elaborate stenciled border below the crown molding balances the dark wainscoting. The crown molding, highlighted with painted details, visually bridges the light and dark borders.

● Stenciling takes a turn to the formal and opulent for the entry of a grand Tudor-style home, *opposite*. Inspired by the paneled mahogany wainscoting and arched door, the stenciled borders recall the tapestries and rich colors of period houses. The lower border echoes the paneled door and adds a hint of fresh green. The border continues, with squared corners, above the wainscoting and cased openings. Walls lighten the look and are mellowed with glaze to avoid harsh contrast.

See page 112 for stencil sources.

GEOMETRICS WITH STYLE. When your goal is to add design interest, consider geometric stenciled motifs as alternatives to more complex designs. Such patterns, often used to repeat, detail plain spaces without taking charge of the decor. You'll be able to find all the classic geometric motifs in commercial stencils. Because the lines and patterns are uncomplicated, you may want to try your hand at making custom stencils. These projects feature both commercial stock stencils and a custom design pattern. Whichever fits your project, select color shades with enough contrast to create interest. See page 93 for further custom directions.

● Echoing the lines of the cast-iron railing, this stylized pattern, *opposite,* details risers in a stair hall. The black accents over the natural oak strengthen the Spanish Colonial ambience of the setting. A tile floor and a tropical palm, potted in a glazed planter, enhance the look. The repetition of black, rather than introducing bright color, unifies the setting and lends a sophisticated note to the decor.

● Stenciled motifs, based on a quilt pattern, *above left,* add the perfect country accent to winding cottage stairs. The gently worn steps, cleaned but not repainted for the project, are the perfect foil for the blocks. Yellow accents repeat the mellow shade of the walls, with touches of green to highlight. **See page 112 for stencil source.**

● Interlocking squares, in pale green and light taupe, create appealing design interest to a painted porch floor, *above right.* The light green painted border emulates a rug and defines the dark green floor. **See page 103 for technique and page 108 for pattern.**

GARDEN-STYLE DELIGHTS. Whatever your decorating style, invite the outdoors inside with charming projects based on stenciled motifs. Turn an empty corner or a back-door work space into a country garden with casual designs, featuring old-fashioned flowers and garden tools. If you prefer a more formal or traditional look, consider the array of topiary and planter motifs reminiscent of chic, well groomed European gardens. Whichever you choose, start the project with a light backdrop in a fresh paint shade appropriate to the outdoors and the garden.

Stenciled over pale yellow walls, the topiary pattern creates a gracious welcome for the entry of an older home, *below.* The light yellow energizes and visually expands the small space while creating a feeling of spring even on cold, wet days. The variety of topiary shapes, stenciled in vertical stripes, along with the period glass sconce with hanging crystals, add interest to the setting.

A commercial stencil with overlays creates the illusion of a watering can casually planted with wildflowers, *above.* Tools, both stenciled and real, enhance the background for this hardworking potting area.

A garden lover's back entry, once a drab mud room, is updated into a cheerful potting shed, *opposite,* with the combination of carefully chosen stencil motifs and the necessary pots and tools. As a start, stenciled wildflowers, chosen for scale and elongated shapes, dress up plain cabinet doors. The watering can and flowers stenciled below the cabinet strengthen the scene. For a decorative display, a salvaged bracket suspends a hanging basket—taking advantage of a sunny window location. Shelves neatly organize pots and tools for potting, and a rustic bench adds additional storage. An old wire egg basket as container and a planter for seed packets are appropriate garden-style finishing touches. **See page 112 for stencil sources.**

Marigold
PERENNIA
ZINNIA

PORCH WITH PIZZAZZ. Consider a plain concrete porch as a blank canvas for your creativity. With paint, stencils, and easy freehand techniques, you can translate a basic setting into a welcoming outdoor area that invites family and friends to enjoy a fresh-air living room.

Lively colors and stenciled motifs transform a plain suburban porch into a well-decorated fresh-air living area, *opposite.* A hand-painted and stenciled "floorcloth" design is actually painted as part of the brightly detailed porch floor, while the ceiling is traditional soft sky blue. Stenciled and hand-painted pillows and terra-cotta pots contribute to the upbeat ambience.

Stylized stamped flowers, detailed with a metallic pen, *above left,* turn plain cotton fabric into stylish accent pillows.

Faux bricks, stamped with a kitchen sponge and detailed for the illusion of grout, *above right,* dress up a porch floor. The terra-cotta color contributes to the realism and adds visual calm.

Decorated with stenciled stars on a green background, the floorcloth features a decorative banded border, courtesy of stamping and handpainting, *left.* Overscaled stenciled flowers and leaves prove the power of paint and bright colors.

See page 104 for technique and page 111 for stencil patterns.

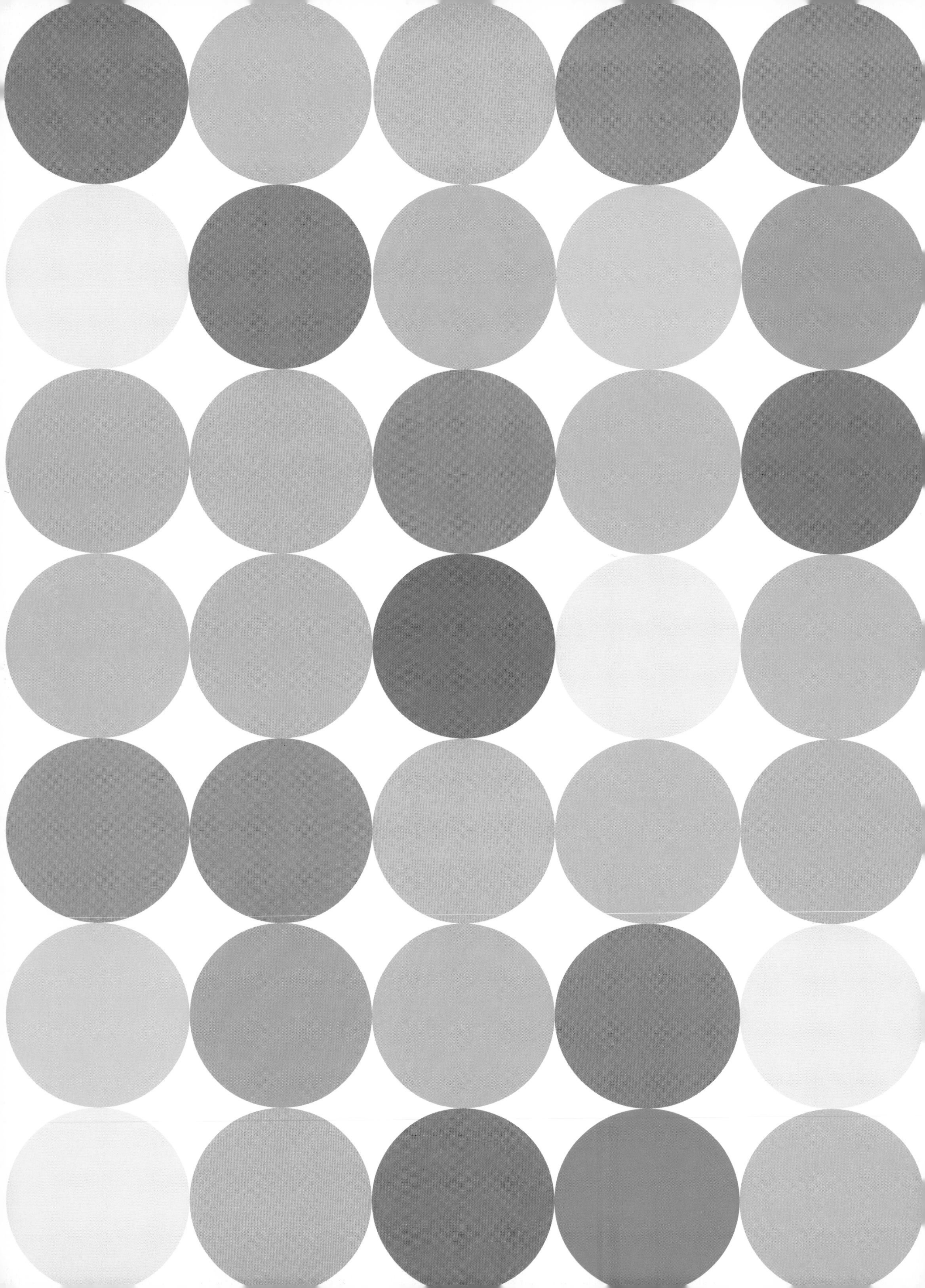

decoratingideas

Express your creativity with stenciling and stamping. The basic techniques for both are easy to learn and offer economical home decorating ideas and solutions. With stenciling and stamping, **projects range from simple to elaborate**—with many variations between. The array of products, from precut stencils to paints to brushes, **creates beautiful, personal effects.** Once you learn the basic techniques, consider projects with overlays (more than one layer of stenciled designs). Or, try your hand at designing and cutting your own stencil or making your own stamp. As the first step, decide on your motif and gather your supplies. **The projects in this book are based on custom designs created for featured projects** or on easily obtainable commercial stencils. **Patterns are on pages 105-111.** Sources for specific featured commercial stencils and directions with supply lists are included in this chapter. **Note that stencil projects are based on single-layer and multiple-layer stencils.** Stamping projects are based on stock and custom-made stamps with specific instructions for each. **For this book, projects are created using acrylics, oil-based stencil paints, and latex wall paints.** Acrylic paints offer the advantage of a range of colors that can be mixed for custom colors. Because they dry quickly, they can be mixed with a commercial extender to prolong the drying time. Each featured project here includes a list of recommended paints and colors with the appropriate brushes and other tools.

For most projects, use a stencil brush, which produces shaded effects. The two basic brushes are soft, domed brushes and stiff, flat-topped brushes. Domed brushes are designed for a swirling or stippling (pouncing the end of the brush) motion. This style of brush works well for most stenciling projects. **Flat-topped brushes are designed just for stippling.** Both styles of brushes come in a variety of sizes from ⅜-inch to 1-inch. You may use a larger brush for overall effect and a smaller one for shading. Use **a separate brush for each color. Practice and surface preparation are crucial to a successful project.** For every project, paint a piece of poster board with your background color, then try the stencil. Adjust the color if necessary. For the actual project, make sure the surface—walls, floors, and furniture—is in good condition. Before you start stenciling, plan the placement of the design. Assemble all the tools and materials. **Measure the surface and lightly mark pinpoint positions that line up with the edge of the stencil.** Attach the stencil, with low-tack masking tape or repositionable spray adhesive, at the first point to be decorated. To use spray adhesive, place the stencil on newspaper with the side to be painted face down. Hold the can about 8 to 12 inches away from the surface and spray a mist to cover the entire stencil back. Use a solvent to remove the excess adhesive if necessary. **Put a small amount of paint onto your palette.** If you are using oil cream paint, remove the skin from the paint and **swirl your brush directly in the paint jar.** If using stencil crayons, rub some crayon on your palette, then swirl your brush in it. Work the paint into the bristles. Swirl the paint on the brush onto a clean part of the palette. Wipe off the excess on scrap paper. Too much paint causes bleeding under the stencil and gives a heavy-looking finish. **Apply paint with a circular or stippling motion** in extremely thin layers, using an almost-dry brush. A cloudy, translucent appearance is the desired effect.

To build up color, apply more layers of paint, allowing drying time between layers. To shade a design, use darker tones for areas in shade and white or a paler shade of the original color for highlights. When the design is completed, remove the stencil. If you missed an area or need extra shading, carefully replace the stencil and touch up as needed.

If you use a stencil with overlays (multiple design sheets), always start with Stencil A and work in alphabetical order. Note that registration lines show where to place the stencils. **Work with one stencil at a time for an entire room or wall.** After the first sheet is stenciled, line up the registration outlines and apply the next overlay (Stencil B). Continue in this orderly fashion. Immediately after finishing, clean brushes used for water-based paint by rinsing under warm, running water. Stencil brush cleaner works well for most stencil paints, even oil-based ones. Towel-dry brushes. To immediately reuse a brush, **finish drying with a hair dryer.** To store, bind a strip of paper towel around the bristles to hold them straight and secure with a rubber band. Let the brushes dry in a warm place and store flat. Also clean stencils immediately after use. If water-based paint has dried, soak the stencil in warm water. Lay the stencil on a flat surface and rub with a damp nylon abrasive pad. Rinse. Clean off oil-based paint with the recommended solvent immediately after use. **Remove spray adhesive** with the solvent recommended. Dry the cleaned stencil with absorbent paper towels, then store flat.

stencil&stamp projects

STENCIL AND STAMPING BASIC SUPPLY LIST

Shop craft and art supply stores for the specialty items needed for stencil and stamp projects. Also consult the listed sources on page 112 for specific stencil companies that sell stencils, supplies, and related items. Home centers and paint stores are also sources. To make your project go as smoothly as possible, stock the following in addition to the listed items under each project's supply list:

- Primer
- Kraft paper
- Tracing paper
- Blue painter's tape
- Low-tack adhesive tape
- Repositionable spray stencil adhesive
- Soft lead pencil
- Colored pencil to match wall
- Scissors
- Level/ruler combination
- Straightedge and tape measure
- Stencil plastic
- Crafts knife
- Extra blades for knife
- Cutting board or self-healing cutting mats
- Small, medium, and large paintbrushes
- Large and medium flat-topped stencil brushes
- Domed stencil brushes in assorted sizes
- Plastic mixing bucket
- Paint tray with liner
- Roller
- Stencil cleaner

KITCHEN AND STAIRWELL FRIEZE

SKILL LEVEL

Intermediate

TIME

Several days

SUPPLIES (IN ADDITION TO THE BASIC SUPPLY LIST)

- Latex wall color (to coordinate with painted wall)

KITCHEN AND STAIRWELL FRIEZE STENCIL

(STENCIL PATTERN ON PAGE 105)

- **An existing pattern in decorative wood trim inspired** the custom-designed stencil. (See page 105 for pattern; see page 93 for how to make a stencil.) To make a stencil from an architectural feature, fabric, or accessory, trace or draw out the pattern, tape it on the wall to look at, then reduce or enlarge it for the most pleasing proportion and scale. Notice where the stencil begins and ends and determine whether you want it to be symmetrical or asymmetrical.
- **Center the stencil and tape in place** with low-tack adhesive. Stencil with latex wall paint. Use a large stencil brush and apply with a pouncing motion. Allow to thoroughly dry. Repeat with several thin coats for opaque coverage.

FAMILY ROOM LATTICE SKILL LEVEL
Advanced
TIME
2 to 3 days
SUPPLIES (IN ADDITION TO THE BASIC SUPPLY LIST)
- Commercial stencil
- White latex paint
- Yellow latex paint
- Black artist's acrylic paint

FIREPLACE MIRROR FRAME SKILL LEVEL
Advanced
TIME
3 days
SUPPLIES (IN ADDITION TO THE BASIC SUPPLY LIST)
- Unpainted frame
- 3 coordinating colors of interior latex paint

FAMILY ROOM LATTICE STENCIL

(STENCIL SOURCE ON PAGE 112)

- **This project features a commercial stencil,** chosen to impart an architectural element relating to the mantel. To create the project, paint the wall above the mantel white.
- Find the center point at the top of the mantel. Starting there, stencil to each side and up. With the stencil in place, paint the negative spaces with the background color (shown warm yellow). Apply paint with a pouncing motion in several coats for opaque coverage.
- Add a touch of black artist's acrylic paint to a small amount of white latex paint to make the light gray for shadows. Mask off shadow areas with blue painter's tape. **Use a small (½-inch) flat-topped brush** to stipple in the shadows. Painting the shadows is a time consuming process, worth the effort to give the lattice the illusion of dimension.

FIREPLACE MIRROR FRAME STENCIL

(STENCIL PATTERN ON PAGE 105)

- **The pattern embossed in the brick surrounding** the firebox translated into the stencil motif for a mirror hung above. To create a stencil from an embossed surface, use tracing paper and a soft lead pencil to make a rubbing from the surface.
- **Size the stencil pattern,** then tape the pattern to a piece of stencil plastic so it can be seen through the plastic. See page 93 for detailed directions for making a stencil. Prime the frame or the surface and lay out the stencil pattern to find the most pleasing composition. See page 105 for the pattern, which includes corners and a connector.
- **Tape the stencil** to the surface and apply paints in a swirling motion. For this project, three colors of latex wall paint were used, based on colors in the adjoining rooms.

GEOMETRIC SCREEN

SKILL LEVEL

Intermediate

TIME

3 days

SUPPLIES (IN ADDITION TO THE BASIC SUPPLY LIST)

- 3 hollow core doors
- 3 colors of latex interior paint, eggshell or satin finish
- Compass
- Low tack masking film or heavy acetate, used to make the stencil

GEOMETRIC SCREEN STENCIL

(STENCIL PATTERN ON PAGE 106)

- **To make a folding screen similar** to one in the featured project, hollow-core doors are primed, painted, and hinged together.
- Measure and mark doors to create a grid as shown. **Tape off and paint** in your choice of background colors. Choose large, graphic stencils in geometric shapes to emulate this clean, contemporary look. If you can't find commercial stencils, make your own basic shapes. See page 93 for directions on making a stencil.
- **Tape on stencils** and stencil with latex paint, applied with a large flat-topped stencil brush. Use a pouncing motion. Apply several coats of paint, allowing to dry thoroughly between coats.

A. For a reverse stencil, use the cutout portion of your stencil pattern.

B. Apply it to the surface, then using a large stencil brush, stipple paint around it.

C. Gently pull off cutout portion of stencil.

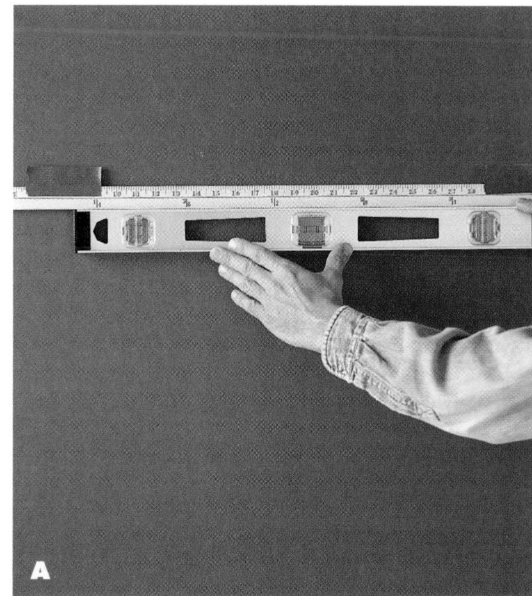

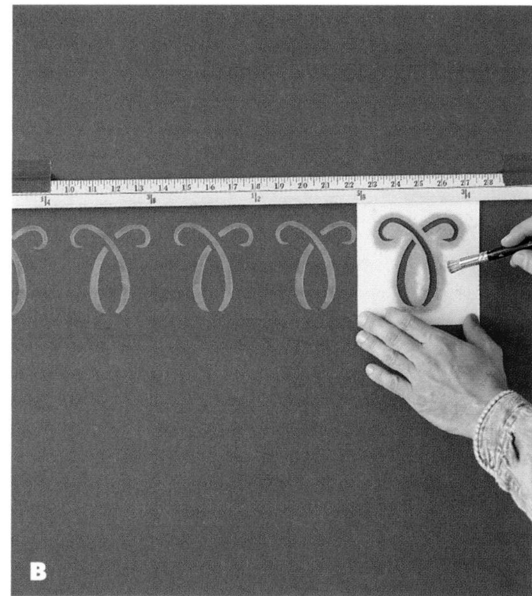

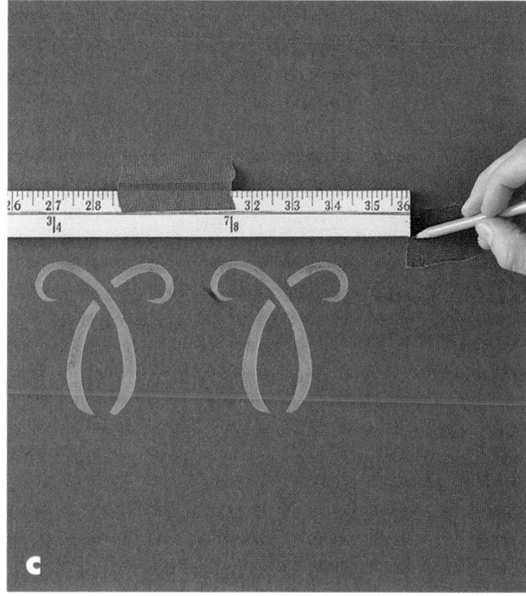

DINING ROOM

SKILL LEVEL

Intermediate

TIME

2 days

SUPPLIES (IN ADDITION TO THE BASIC SUPPLY LIST)

- Drawing paper
- Gold-tone metallic oil-based stencil paint
- Leftover wall paint (to match wall color)
- Cotton or linen slipcovers

DINING ROOM STENCIL

(STENCIL PATTERN ON PAGE 105)

- **For this project, the curves of the chandelier and fabric motif inspired** the stencil. For the borders, position one row of stenciling at chair-rail height (approximately 36 inches) and one row slightly below the height of the doorway.

A. Determine height of border, then level the straightedge and tape in place.

B. Use the level straightedge as a guide for positioning the stencil across the wall.

C. At the end of the straightedge, place a piece of tape and mark it with the pencil. Use this point to extend and level the straightedge across the wall.

- **Use leftover paint from walls** (or a similar color) to stencil the slipcovers. Wash or dry clean fabric before stenciling.
- **Practice on a similar fabric** before attempting slipcovers. Apply paint in a swirling motion with a small stencil brush for both projects. To allow the stenciled slipcovers to be washed, check with an art supply store on a conditioner that can be added to wall paint.

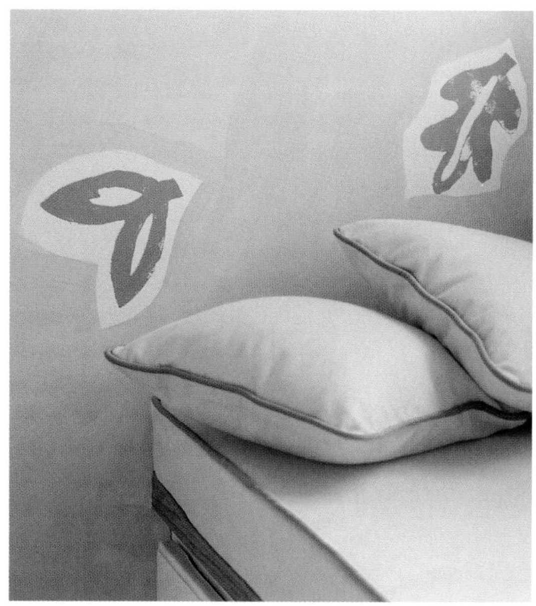

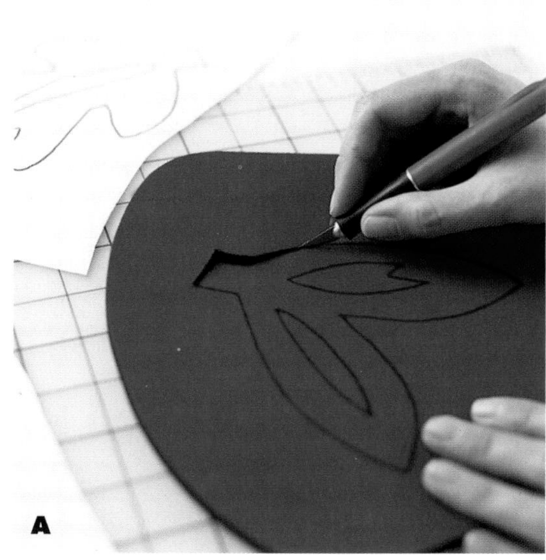

A

STAMPED LEAF GIRL'S ROOM
SKILL LEVEL
Intermediate
TIME
2 days
SUPPLIES (IN ADDITION TO THE BASIC SUPPLY LIST)

- White latex paint (if walls are repainted for project)
- 2 computer mouse pads
- Stencil painter roller or similar foam roller
- Acrylic paint (1 quart each)
  - Dark periwinkle
  - Dark pink
  - Medium pink
  - Medium intensity Lime green
- 1 quart decorators' glaze

STAMPED LEAF GIRL'S ROOM

(STAMP PATTERN ON PAGE 105)

■ **Choose a fresh, upbeat color scheme.** Directions are given for the colors featured. You can create your own look based on fabric or accessories. Choose a motif for the stamp. The motif shown is based on the comforter fabric. This project begins with white walls.

■ **To make a rubber stamp,** choose a simple design. Draw the motif on paper and cut out. This project features two stamps, measuring 8 inches long and 6 inches long.

A. Trace around the design onto a mouse pad; cut out with a crafts knife.

B. Roll paint onto the stamp with roller. Apply the stamp to the wall in a random pattern, leaving room for other stamps. Stamp additional leaf shapes for a visually interesting mix of color.

C. Finish by glazing the walls. Mix lime green glaze with a glaze-to-paint ratio of 3 to 1. Brush the glaze onto the wall, leaving white space around each stamp. Cover all other wall areas. Work quickly and avoid leaving hard edges that could dry and resemble lines. If you have to stop, brush out (feather) the lines where you stop. This softens the glaze edges. The amount of glaze/paint mixture needed for a medium-size room is a little more than a quart.

B

C

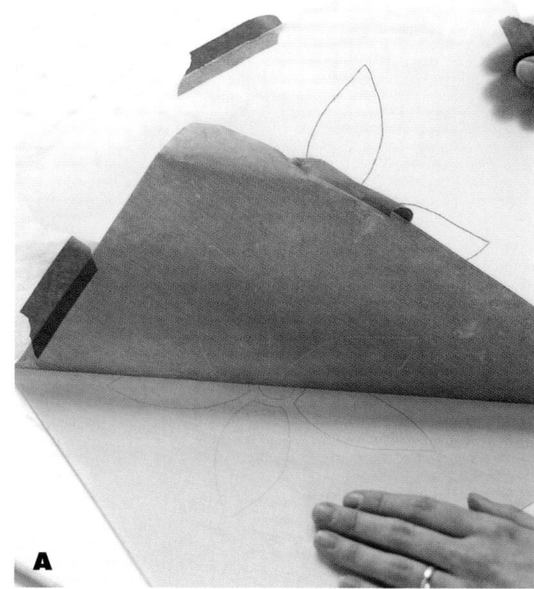

A

STENCILED FLOWER GIRL'S ROOM
SKILL LEVEL
Intermediate
TIME
2 days
SUPPLIES (IN ADDITION TO THE BASIC SUPPLY LIST)
- Graphite or carbon paper
- Fine-tipped marker
- Bright lavender/periwinkle latex wall paint
- White stencil paint

STENCILED FLOWER GIRL'S ROOM
(STENCIL PATTERN ON PAGE 106)

- **The appliquéd sheer window covering fabric inspired this garden-fresh flower border.** Choose a motif as shown or draw your own, simplifying the design so that it can be made into a stencil. Make sure that design elements are not too large or shaped in a way that makes stenciling difficult. When you are satisfied with the design, transfer it to stencil material.
- **If you use** translucent stencil plastic, place the pattern underneath the stencil plastic and trace with a fine-tipped marker. If the plastic isn't large enough, tape two pieces together.

A. Use graph paper or carbon paper to transfer the pattern to opaque stencil board or poster board. Cut out the stencil design with a crafts knife. Be sure to have extra blades on hand and switch to sharp blades as often as necessary. Always cut on a cutting board. (Self-healing cutting mats are available at arts and crafts stores.)

B. Roll stencil back onto itself to trace part of the pattern for registration marks.

C. Place stencil just below ceiling at the top of the wall. Stipple lightly in white paint with a medium-size brush. Line up the registration pattern and continue stenciling across wall.

B

C

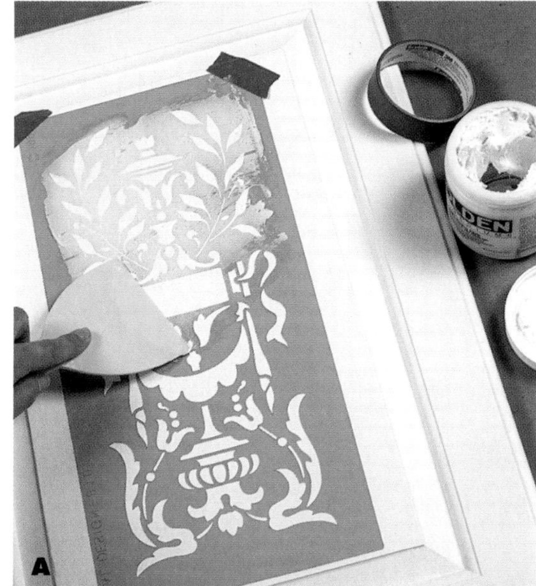

TRADITIONAL BEAUTY

SKILL LEVEL

Advanced

TIME

3 days

SUPPLIES (IN ADDITION TO THE BASIC SUPPLY LIST)

- Commercial stencil
- Golden's hard molding paste
- Trowel
- Metal paint pan
- 2 pan liners
- Fine sandpaper
- Black latex paint
- Metallic silver paint
- Black antique glaze
- Cheesecloth
- Natural bristle brush

TRADITIONAL BEAUTY

(STENCIL SOURCE ON PAGE 112)

- **This project features a commercial stencil.** When starting a dimensional stenciling project, use a repositioning spray adhesive to keep larger stencils stationary while you work. To affix the stencil, hold the spray adhesive can at least 12 inches away from the stencil, lightly misting the back to ensure a tight seal around the edges of the design. Wait one minute for it to set before attaching to the surface

A. To create the three-dimensional design, trowel a textured material over and through the stencil. Gently work it into all the open areas. Hold the trowel at an oblique (almost parallel) angle to the surface and apply light pressure to the surface.

- **For a more pronounced relief**, build up a thicker layer of the material as before to completely cover the stencil. Carefully remove the stencil by lifting immediately from one corner. If edges form around the design, sand when dry with fine sandpaper.

Allow the relief to dry. Roll on two coats of black latex paint to fully cover. Allow to dry.

- **To create a jeweled look,** apply a solid coat of metallic silver paint to simulate silver leaf. Allow the paint to thoroughly dry.

B. Distress the cabinet door by lightly sanding the surface with fine-grade sandpaper.

C. Apply black antique glaze to accent the relief. With a cheesecloth, rub off most of the antique glaze. Allow some paint to remain in the crevices to accentuate the dimensional effect.

A

VINTAGE PATTERN ALL-OVER WALL

SKILL LEVEL

Advanced

TIME

4 days

SUPPLIES (IN ADDITION TO THE BASIC SUPPLY LIST)

- Commercial stencils
- Off-white latex paint
- Yellow latex paint
- Glaze
- Paintbrush
- 2 clean metal paint cans for mixing glazes
- Clean cotton rags
- Golden sienna acrylic

VINTAGE PATTERN ALL-OVER WALL STENCIL

(STENCIL SOURCE ON PAGE 112)

■ **This tone-on-tone** combination uses an all-over damask pattern laid between stripes created by a vertically stenciled border. This creates the look of custom wallpaper with a painterly quality .

■ **For the background, paint walls off-white.** Mix yellow glaze in a ratio of three parts glaze to 1 part paint. Roll on glaze and rag off with a clean cotton rag to create a subtle texture. Determine the layout of the striped border and the width of the all-over pattern in between.

A. Use a level to measure and mark off plumb guidelines. Draw light pencil lines.

B. Tape off the areas for the border stripes and apply a second layer of glaze to deepen the tone.

C. When dry, reposition tape. Add golden sienna to the glaze to deepen and create a new color. Use this glaze to stencil the stripe/border design. Stencil all-over damask pattern in between using the same color.

■ **When stenciling with glazes,** be sure to remove excess paint by wiping the brush on absorbent paper towels. This prevents the glaze from leaking under the stencils. For a more distressed, aged look, stencil using random pressure to allow the color to fade away in places as you stencil.

B

C

GARDEN COTTAGE LIVING ROOM
SKILL LEVEL
Advanced
TIME
3 days
SUPPLIES (IN ADDITION TO THE BASIC SUPPLY LIST)
- Felt-tip marker
- Tapered brush
- Medium yellow latex wall paint
- White latex wall paint
- Decorators' glaze
- Acrylic stencil paints

GARDEN COTTAGE DINING ROOM
SKILL LEVEL
Advanced
TIME
2 days
SUPPLIES (IN ADDITION TO THE BASIC SUPPLY LIST)
- Geranium stencil
- Decorators' glaze
- Acrylic stencil paints
- Tapered 2-inch brush
- White and blue latex wall paint

GARDEN COTTAGE LIVING ROOM STENCIL

- **Design and create the backdrop** for stenciled motifs. Paint the wall medium yellow. Allow to dry. Measure and determine the size for the rectangles. (Rectangles shown are 12x16 inches.) Lightly draw in the outlines of the rectangle with a level, ruler, and colored pencil that is similar to the background color.
- **Mix the whitewash** with a ratio of 3 parts glaze to 1 part white paint. Paint with a tapered brush. Design simple stencils with no more than two overlays to each stencil. Choose motifs from a print fabric for a pleasant mix of elements. If you draw, sketch simple shapes. Or photocopy motifs from the fabric and alter the scale on the photocopier to fit the space.
- **Alternately, trace designs** directly from the fabric onto tracing paper, scale up or down with a photocopier and convert into stencils. See page 93 for directions on designing and cutting stencils. For example, design a light green leaf shape with darker green accents. Trace and cut out the stencils. Center the stencil motifs inside every other rectangle.

GARDEN COTTAGE DINING ROOM STENCIL

(STENCIL SOURCE ON PAGE 112)

- **For this project,** glazed walls create cottage ambience. First paint the walls white, allow to dry. Brush blue glaze over the white in a ratio of three parts glaze to one part blue paint. Using a level and blue pencil, lightly draw guidelines for horizontal stripe (here 6½ inches high) below the plate rail.
- **Tape off lines** with blue painter's tape; paint white. Allow to dry. Stencil the motif pictured in this project with water-based paint. Stencil the geranium bloom in pale yellow, then stencil darker yellow to the edges. Add peach highlights. Stencil stems with dark green stencil paint. Stencil leaves with a lighter green. Add dark blue to the leaf edges for detailing and accents.

COTTAGE TULIP WALL SKILL LEVEL

Advanced

TIME

4 days

SUPPLIES (IN ADDITION TO THE BASIC SUPPLY LIST)

- Commercial stencil
- Pale blue latex paint
- Pale green and blue latex paint
- Decorators' glaze
- Oil-based blue and green stencil paint

COTTAGE TULIP FLOORCLOTH SKILL LEVEL

Intermediate

TIME

4 days

- Commercial stencil
- Floorcloth material
- Leak-proof dropcloth
- Green and blue latex paint
- No. 10 round artist's brushes
- White latex paint
- Medium blue and green stencil paints
- Cotton cloths
- Water-based polyurethane
- Spray-on backing

GARDEN COTTAGE TULIP WALL STENCIL

(STENCIL SOURCE ON PAGE 112)

■ **This project incorporates a commercial tulip stencil** chosen to complement the appliqued tulips on the sheer fabric. Walls are decoratively painted for a pretty backdrop. Paint the room white, choosing satin or eggshell sheen. With a level and either a light blue or light green colored pencil, draw a series of vertical lines every 10½ inches, starting in a corner and working around the room. Striping two or three walls saves time while creating a pretty backdrop.

■ **Tape to the left** of every line with 2-inch-wide blue painter's tape and smooth down the tape edges. Roll on a thin layer of neutral (untinted) decorators' glaze to seal the edges of the tape. This prevents the blue and green stripes from bleeding under the tape.

■ **After all the tape** is in place, use a small roller to paint every other stripe blue; then paint the remaining stripes green. Allow to dry. Carefully remove the tape, revealing the white stripes.

■ **Remove the pattern** from the stencil package. Cut apart the paper stencil image and tape to the wall to determine tulip stencil placement.

■ **This stencil comes as a row of tulips.** Cut apart for easy maneuvering and use individual tulips.

■ **Stencil tulips** around the room, keeping furniture placement in mind. Use medium blue stencil paint for petals; concentrate paint on some edges or add a darker or lighter blue for interest. Use green for leaves; concentrate for shadows. Apply paint with a pouncing motion, using a medium brush. Use all three overlays for each tulip.

GARDEN COTTAGE TULIP FLOORCLOTH STENCIL

(STENCIL SOURCE ON PAGE 112)

■ **For an easy project, purchase floor cloth material**, rather than canvas. See source on page 112. Cut the floorcloth to the size you desire. To cut the oval shape, find and mark the center of each side of the rectangular floorcloth. Draw the oval curve onto one-fourth of the rug.

■ **When you are satisfied** with the curve, cut out in one piece. Use this piece as a pattern to trace onto the other three-quarters of the rug. Cut the remaining sides. Draw a scalloped border around the edge and cut with scissors. Place rug on a leak-proof dropcloth. Prime. Using a small roller, paint the entire rug with green latex paint.

■ **Allow the base coat** to dry. Recoat if necessary. Paint a blue border onto the rug to mimic the scalloped pattern. With a No. 10 round artist's brush, paint a thin white line that mimics the blue scalloped edge.

■ Tape tulip pattern samples to determine placement on the floorcloth. Stencil tulips as directed for the tulip wall stencil. Allow to dry. Seal immediately with a water-based polyurethane protector. Apply two to three coats for durability. Coat the back with a rubber backing available in an aerosol spray. Allow to dry before placing on the floor.

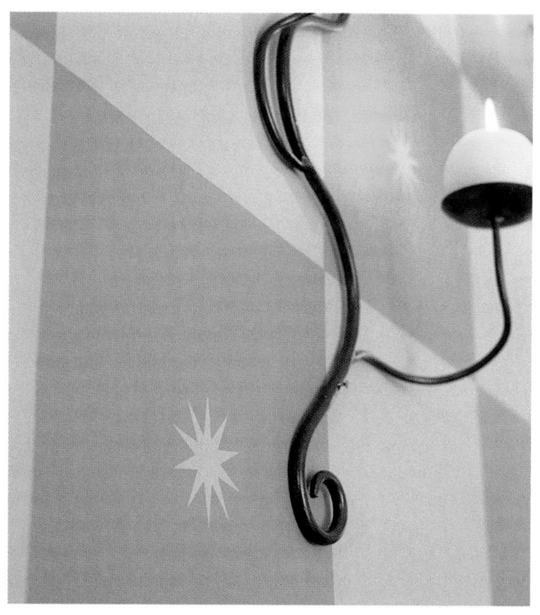

CHECKERBOARD FIREPLACE WALL
SKILL LEVEL
Beginner
TIME
1 day
SUPPLIES (IN ADDITION TO THE BASIC SUPPLY LIST)
- 2 colors of interior latex paint
- Commercial stencil

MARTINI TIME ROOM
SKILL LEVEL
Intermediate
TIME
2 days
SUPPLIES (IN ADDITION TO THE BASIC SUPPLY LIST)
- Latex paint
- Compressed sponge
- Acrylic stencil paints:
  - Medium green
  - Dark green
  - Dark red for pimiento
  - Navy blue
  - Lighter blue

CHECKERBOARD FIREPLACE WALL STENCIL

(STENCIL SOURCE ON PAGE 112)

- **This project features the two colors of the living room.** Paint the background with the darker of two colors. Measure the wall space and determine dimensions of squares. Measure; then mark off squares using a level and pencil. Tape off with painter's tape.
- **Paint lighter squares** and remove the tape. Determine placement of the stars. The stars shown are stenciled on the darker squares. Tape the stencil in place. Apply the lighter of the two colors with a pouncing motion.

MARTINI TIME ROOM STENCIL

(STENCIL PATTERN ON PAGE 107)

- **Use the patterns** on page 107 to make the martini glass stencil and the olive stamps. See page 93, Stenciled Girl's Room, for detailed directions on making your own stencils. Paint the background, if repainting. Cut stencil and stencil the martini glass in dark blue. Make a second stencil for the drink line and stencil in light blue as shown. See page 92, Stamped Girl's Room, for directions on making stamps.
- **Follow the patterns** to make the olive and pimiento stamps, which are made from compressed sponge material, available at arts and crafts store. Trace the pattern onto the sponge, cut it out with a pair of sharp scissors or a crafts knife, and expand with water.
- **Place a small amount** of each color of liquid acrylic on a paper plate and dip the sponges into the paint. Blot the sponges onto paper to remove excess paint. Randomly stamp the olives on the wall. Stamp olive over martini glasses as you desire for a lively effect.

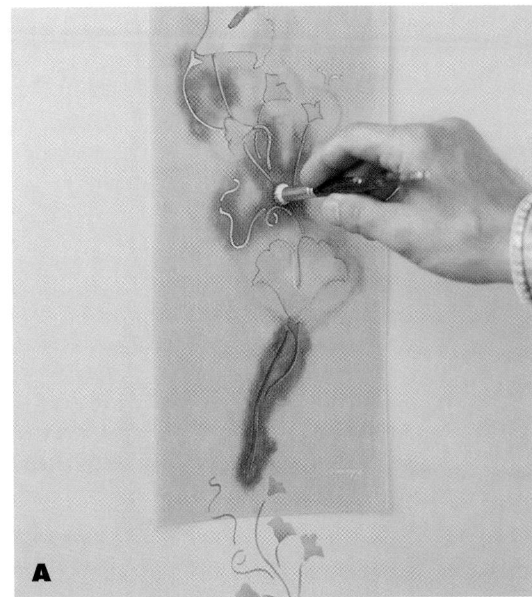

A

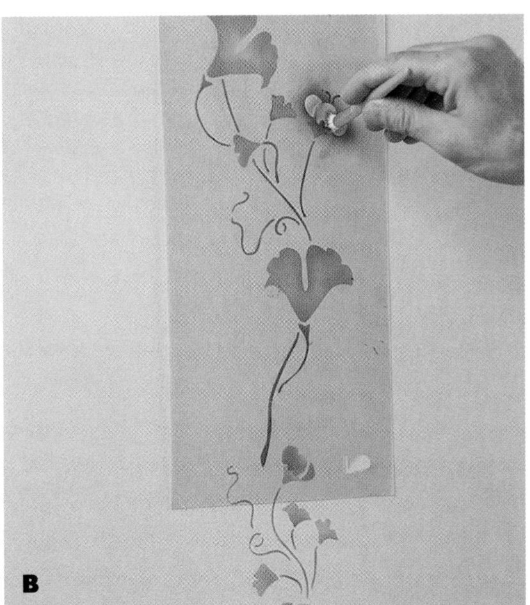

B

GINKGO COUNTRY LIVING ROOM
SKILL LEVEL
Intermediate
TIME
1½ days
SUPPLIES (IN ADDITION TO THE BASIC SUPPLY LIST)
- Yellow latex paint if repainting wall
- Ginkgo leaf commercial stencil with overlays
- Oil-based stencil paints:
  - Olive green
  - Dark green
  - Brown

GINKGO COUNTRY LIVING ROOM STENCIL
(STENCIL SOURCE ON PAGE 112)

- **This project features stencil overlays,** which are used for more detailing. When you use commercial overlays, carefully follow the directions.
- **Always begin with Stencil A** and work alphabetically. After the first sheet is stenciled around the room, match the registration outlines and stencil second overlay (Stencil B). For best results, pay careful attention to stenciling around doorways.
- **Start at the top left hand side of the door frame.** (The leaves should point up and away from the woodwork.) Stencil down to the baseboard. Apply the second color to stems and areas to be shaded for a natural look.

If the stencil run doesn't end in a complete pattern, choose where to end the stencil. Do not stencil half a leaf, for example; rather, stop at the most attractive point.

A. Position first stencil. Apply one paint color to leaves. Apply the second paint color to the stems and areas to be shaded.

B. Line up second overlay with pattern on the wall. Stencil remaining details. Continue with additional overlays, if applicable. Stencil above the baseboard with leaves pointing down.

- **Wash the stencil.** See page 87 for tips. To stencil the right side of the door frame, flip the stencil over and keep leaves pointing up and away from the frame.

A

MONKEYS ON PATROL

SKILL LEVEL

Advanced

TIME

2 days

SUPPLIES (IN ADDITION TO THE BASIC SUPPLY LIST)

- Graphite paper if needed
- Large piece of acetate
- Brown or tan acrylic paint
- Dark brown acrylic paint
- Red acrylic paint
- Brushes

MONKEYS ON PATROL STENCIL

(STENCIL PATTERN ON PAGE 108)

- **Enlarge the stencil** to a scale appropriate to your room. Use an oversize copier at a copy center. Trace the monkey outline onto stencil plastic, a large piece of poster board, or acetate. Cut out the monkey outline with a crafts knife; label it Stencil A.
- **Trace the monkey details**. Details include eyes, hair, and toes. Make a stencil for the details by tracing over the pattern and enlarging. Trace details onto stencil material. Draw the outline of the monkey onto the stencil so you will know where to lay the stencil when you are ready. Cut out the details only. Label this Stencil B. Make a stencil for the ball. Cut out.

A Place Stencil A, the monkey shape, onto the wall. Place it in a spot where the monkey will appear to be hanging from a vine. (The vine will be added later.)

- **Stencil this first overlay** in a solid medium brown or tan.

B Use darker brown to shade outline of monkey.

C After giving the outline enough time to dry, place Stencil B on top, lining it up so all the details are positioned correctly. Stencil these details in a dark brown.

- **Stencil the red ball** in the monkey's paw.

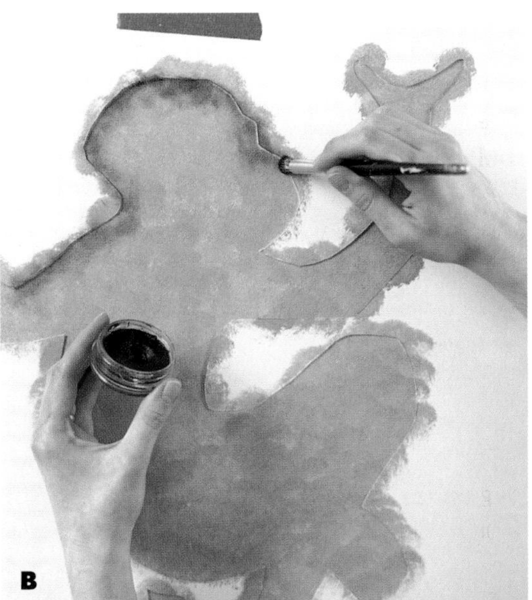

B

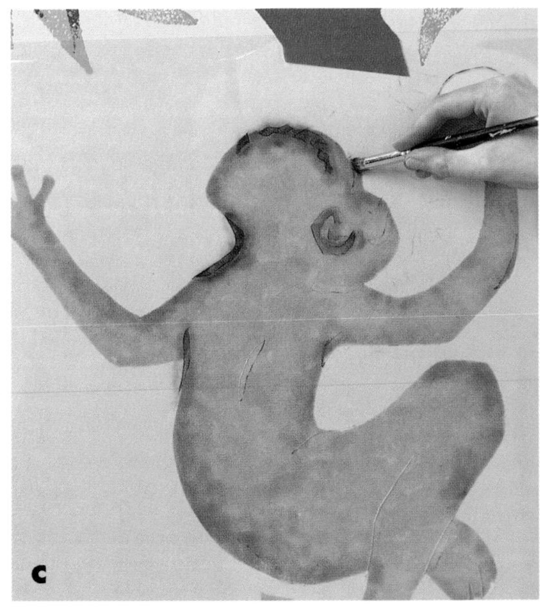

C

VINES AND FRONDS
SKILL LEVEL
Intermediate
TIME
1½ days
SUPPLIES (IN ADDITION TO THE BASIC SUPPLY LIST)

- Compressed sponge for leaves
- Pen to trace patterns onto sponge
- Two medium values of green
- One dark value of green
- Plate or paint tray
- Stencil plastic or acetate
- Medium and dark values of brown stencil paints

VINES AND PALM FRONDS
(STENCIL PATTERN ON PAGE 108)

- **For the palm fronds and branches,** begin by drawing branch shapes onto a large piece of paper. Use simple curved shapes and determine the length of branches you would like to use for the particular space, making several sizes, with ends curved in different directions. (See page 93 for detailed directions on making stencils.)
- **Stencil these branches** into place with brown paint, leaving enough room for leaves on each side of the branches. Trace leaf shapes onto the compressed sponge and cut out with scissors. Enlarge leaf shapes with water and wring out.

A. Pour a medium green paint color into a plate or paint tray. Dip sponge into paint and blot.

- **Sponge the fronds along the branches**, overlapping and moving in slightly different directions. Make them appear as they would in a natural jungle setting.

B. Sponge second medium green color for additional leaves to work with the wall space.

C. Add dark green accents. Repeat for all branches.

D. At this point, stencil monkey (see page 100). To add vine for monkey, tape a large piece of acetate to the wall, over the monkey. Draw a vine onto the acetate placed to appear as if the monkey were perched on it. Draw so the vine disappears into the palm branches or the ceiling. Cut out vines. Stencil in a medium to dark brown with darker brown shadows.

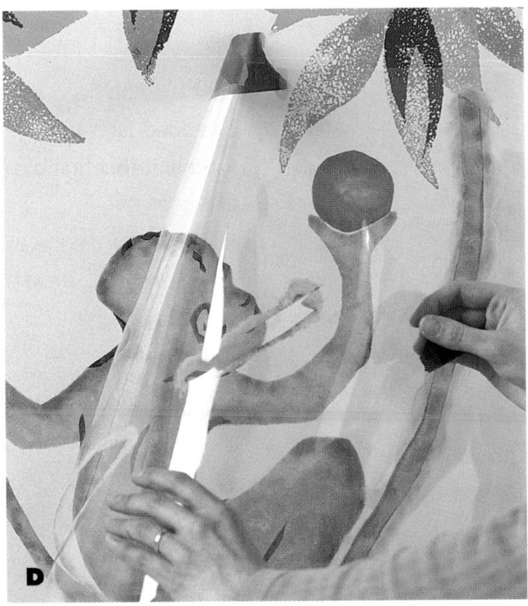

DOG AND CAT NURSERY SKILL LEVEL
Intermediate

TIME
4 days

SUPPLIES (IN ADDITION TO THE BASIC SUPPLY LIST)
- White latex paint
- Satin-finish paint, 1 quart each: red, green, aqua, blue, black
- 2 quarts satin-finish yellow paint
- Glaze
- Heavy-weight acetate
- Sea sponges
- 2-inch brush

BUNNY NURSERY SKILL LEVEL
Intermediate

TIME
5 days

SUPPLIES
- Self-adhesive paper
- Satin-finish paint 1 quart each: light, medium, dark green; 1 quart each: pale pink, peach, hot pink, lavender, purple, black
- Glaze
- Acetate
- Sea sponges

DOG AND CAT NURSERY STENCIL

(STENCIL PATTERNS ON PAGE 109)

- **See page 109 for stencils custom-designed for this project.** See pages 93 and 100 for directions on copying patterns and making your own stencils. If you prefer to purchase commercial stencils, see page 112 for sources.
- **Paint the walls** for background.
- **Measure the walls** and determine the placement of the stencils. Cut out stencil patterns and experiment with placement before stenciling. Space the squares with the motif around the room. Using a level with ruler, mark the placement of the squares. Stencil the border for each square.
- **When the border is dry,** tape the motifs—dog, cat, bone, and paw prints—in the center of each square. Dab the sea sponge in a tiny bit of glaze then into the paint color, blot and cover the area evenly with a blotting motion. Use one sea sponge for each color. After the motifs are dry, use a small round artist's brush to add details.
- **Allow squares with motifs** to dry completely. Above and below motifs, measure 6-inch-wide stripes and lightly draw guide lines. Mask off stripes with painter's tape. Loosely brush on yellow paint with a two-inch brush. Dip a sea sponge in glaze and blot over painted stripes to soften the effect.

BUNNY IN THE GARDEN NURSERY STENCIL

(STENCIL PATTERNS ON PAGE 110)

- **See page 110 for stencil patterns.** See pages 93 and 100 for directions on copying patterns and making your own stencils. For a pleasing placement of motifs, cut out paper patterns of the stencils and tape to the wall before you begin. Determine the size of the fence pickets based on the size of the room. The pickets in this project measure 4 inches wide by 28 inches high. Cut fence pickets from self-adhesive paper. Position on the wall. Dab sea sponge in glaze, then green paint. Sponge between the pickets to create the grass. When the glaze is dry, remove paper and hand-paint dark green nail details.
- **For vegetables,** tape patterns to the walls to determine positions. Hand-paint wavy lines for peas and vines. Tape stencil and stencil vegetables. For the soft, painterly effect of this project, dab a sea sponge in glaze, then hand-paint in a blotting motion over the stencil. When dry, paint loose green detail swirls.
- **Outline the bunny by hand** with a pencil, copying the photographs. Loosely paint the outline. (Practice first on scrap paper to be sure of the effect.) After all the motifs are painted, detailed, and dry, mix the background glaze: one part lavender, one part white, two parts glaze. With a loose, freehand motion, brush the glaze onto the wall. Blend and soften with a sea sponge dipped in glaze.

MOSAIC TILE
SKILL LEVEL
Intermediate
TIME
1½ days
SUPPLIES (IN ADDITION TO THE BASIC SUPPLY LIST)

- Yellow latex wall paint
- Commercial stencil
- Oil-based stencil paint: purple and green

INTERLOCKING SQUARES
SKILL LEVEL
Beginner
TIME
2 days
SUPPLIES (IN ADDITION TO THE BASIC SUPPLY LIST)

- 3 colors of water-based porch paint
- Water-based sealer

MOSAIC TILE BORDER STENCIL

(STENCIL SOURCE ON PAGE 112)

- **For this project,** use a commercial stencil with two overlays. First stencil in the square overlay at the four corners of the window outside the trim. Then stencil in the overlay that emulates waves.
- **Keep the waves moving** in one direction around the window and above the tile. Stencil the main part of the overlay in purple; stencil the center in green, as shown.

INTERLOCKING SQUARES STENCIL

(STENCIL PATTERN ON PAGE 108)

- **The interlocking squares stencil pattern** works well for porch floors because of its simplicity. If you would like to try other motifs, see additional porch floor pattern on page 112; see page 93 to make your own stencil.
- **As a first step,** paint the porch floor with water-based porch paint. Allow to thoroughly dry. Mask a 12-inch border with blue painter's tape. With the second shade of water-based paint, paint around the porch perimeter for the impression of an area rug. Place the stencil randomly, reminiscent of old linoleum patterns. Using water-based floor paint, stencil with a medium-size brush in a pouncing motion. Apply the overlay the same way. Allow to dry. Seal with a water-based sealer for durability.

PORCH WITH PIZZAZZ
SKILL LEVEL
Intermediate
TIME
3 days
SUPPLIES (IN ADDITION TO THE BASIC SUPPLY LIST)

- Commercial concrete etcher
- Xylene (for cleaning brushes)
- Silicon acrylic Concrete stain in light buff, brick red, seafoam green, and Caribbean blue
- 2-inch-wide masking tape
- Pierced leaf stencil
- Pierced and solid rose stencil
- Four 14-inch by 16-inch sheets of acetate
- 5 foam plates
- Artist liner brush (10/0 size)
- 2-inch paint brush

PORCH WITH PIZZAZZ
(STENCIL PATTERNS ON PAGE 111)

Note: The project was designed for a concrete porch; however, the motifs translate to wood porches. (See page 103 for more information on painting wood porches.) If you work on concrete, scrape and pressure wash it to remove debris. Acid-wash concrete with a commercial concrete etcher according to manufacturer's directions, using a push broom and watering can. Follow ALL SAFETY PRECAUTIONS. Wear safety goggles and cover plantings with plastic. Let the clean concrete dry for 72 hours.

- **Paint the entire porch** light buff according to the manufacturer's directions. If you paint only roses, continue with the following directions. If you paint the rug motif, as shown in the featured project, tape off the outer perimeter of the desired rug size now. Do not paint in the taped off area. Let dry 24 hours. To continue with the rug, remove the tape and then tape off a 5-inch border; paint the border blue. Let dry 24 hours and tape off the center of the rug. Paint it seafoam green. Clean rollers.
- **Enlarge or reduce stencil** patterns to fit the space. For sizing, first photocopy stencils from this book and size up or down on a photocopier.
- **Follow the directions for tracing and cutting** stencils on page 93. Cut out stencils with stencil plastic and a crafts knife. Note that the rose is made with an outline stencil and an overlay for the details. See monkey stencil project, page 100, for more information on tracing, cutting, and working with detail overlays.
- **Randomly lay out the solid rose stencil** on the porch floor, marking the outline with a pencil to be sure of placement. Spray stencil adhesive to the back of the stencil and place the stencil over the pencil outline. Pour brick red paint into an aluminum plate. With a 2-inch paint brush, fill in with brick red paint, working quickly. Do not over brush. Dry 24 hours.
- **Place the stencil** for the rose details over the solid painted rose. Use spray adhesive to hold in place. Mix one part brick red and one part light buff in a foam plate. Pour light buff into a second foam plate. With an artist liner brush, first dip the brush into a generous amount of the mixed paint, then directly into the solid buff paint. Without mixing paints, swipe along the pierced stencil's opening. Reapply paints to brush as needed, alternating the colors.
- **To add definition to each rose,** dip the liner brush into the mixed paint and loosely trace a shadow line of paint around the stenciled line and intermittently around the perimeter.
- **For leaves,** make the solid leaf stencil. Trace the stencil into varying positions around the roses, penciling in two or three leaves per rose. Fill in solid leaf stencil with seafoam green; dry 24 hours. Mix equal amounts of seafoam green and light buff and stencil the leaf overlay over the solid leaves. Dry 24 hours. For the rug, make the star stencil and stencil randomly in light buff on the seafoam background. Use an artist's brush to paint a wavy seafoam green line on the Caribbean blue rug border. Randomly add light buff dots between the wavy lines.

KITCHEN AND STAIRWELL FRIEZE STENCIL

FIREPLACE MIRROR FRAME STENCIL

DINING ROOM STENCIL

STAMPED LEAF GIRL'S ROOM

STAMPED LEAF GIRL'S ROOM

GEOMETRIC SCREEN STENCIL

GEOMETRIC SCREEN STENCIL DIAGRAM

STENCILED FLOWER GIRL'S ROOM

MONKEYS ON PATROL PALM FRONDS STENCIL
MARTINI TIME ROOM STENCIL

MONKEYS ON PATROL BALL STENCIL

MONKEYS ON PATROL STENCIL OUTLINE OVERLAY AND BASE

INTERLOCKING SQUARES STENCIL WITH REGISTRATION MARKS

DOG AND CAT NURSERY STENCIL

BUNNY IN THE GARDEN NURSERY STENCIL

PORCH WITH PIZZAZZ STENCIL

SOURCES AND CREDITS:

Pages 8-9, 20-39: Melanie Royal, Royal Design Studio, 2504 Transportation Ave., Ste. H, National City, CA 91950; 800/747-9767; www.royaldesignstudio.com
Pages 10-19, 40-55, 58-63, 68-75, 78-81: Wade Scherrer and Patricia Mohr Kramer
Pages 56-57, 64-67: Tina Blanck Inc., 639 W. 57th Terrace, Kansas City, MO 64113; telephone/fax: 816/333-1517
Pages 76-77: Susan Goan Driggers and Staff of Paint Décor magazine
Pages 82-83: Amy Queen, Missouri City, TX; 281/321-7333
Plaid Enterprises Inc.,Norcross, GA 30091; 800/842-4197; www.plaidonline.com
Design Stencils, 2503 Silverside Road, Wilmington, DE 19810, 800/822-7836
Calico Corners, 800/213-6366; www.calicocorners.com
Whittier Wood Products, P.O. Box 2827, Eugene, OR 97402. For dealers, 800/653-3336
Photography: 10-19, 40-55, 58-63, 68-75, 78-81, 86-93, 96-111, 103: Pete Krumhardt
Pages 8-9, 34-39: Colleen Duffley
Pages 21-33, 94-95: Ed Gohlich
Pages 56-57, 64-67, 102: Bob Greenspan
Pages 84-85, 104: Fran Brennan
Page 15: Stencil Décor, Garden Lattice.
Pages 16-17: Lamp: Target Stores
Pages 18-19: Fabric: Summer Garden; Calico Corners; lamp: Target Stores: 800/800-8800
Pages 20-21: Stencils: 19th Century Ivy, Bitty Borders, Floral Fancy, Royal Design Studio
Pages 22-23: Basketweave, Hydraneas, Peony Rose, Sweetheart Ivy, Morning Glories, Grapevine Twigs, Poppies, Royal Design Studio
Pages 24-25: Grapevine Trellis, Grape Clusters, Peony Rose, Trailing Along, Royal Design Studio
Pages 26-27: Fabric Damask, Reverse Scroll, Floral Chain, Florentine Grille, Royal Design
Pages 28-29: Renaissance Tile series: European Lace Medallion, European Lace Corner, European Lace Center, Large Scroll All-over, Small Florentine Grille, Oriental Brushstroke, Florence, Palermo, Verona Tile, Royal Design
Pages 30-31: Stencils: Large Ribbon Trellis, Wisteria, Small Shell Overlay, Royal Design
Pages 32-33: Stencils: Micah, Toulouse, Parisian Swag, Parisian Urn, Royal Design.
Pages 34-39: Stencils: Royal Design Studio
Pages 40-41: Stencil: Small Endless Acanthus Swirl, Royal Design Studio:
Pages 42-43: Designer Stencils: S4-2694-08, 800/822-7836.
Pages 44-45: Bamboo shades: Smith+Noble; 800/248-8888; smithandnoble.com
Pages 46-47: Fabric: Mayflowers (Sunshine); Pretty Plaid (Sunshine); Seasonings (Primrose); Spring Morning (Sunshine); Waverly: 800/423-5881; armoire: Whittier Wood Products
Pages 50-51: Stencils: Geranium, 10-158-08 and Butterfly, 2693; Designer Stencils; table and chairs courtesy of Whittier Wood Products
Pages 52-53: Stencil: Gingko, 19-2039-25 (twig and vine collection), Designer Stencils; slipcover fabric: Ricola (Sage); courtesy of Calico Corners
Page 54: Stencil: Olive Branch, 19-2071-25, Designer Stencils
Page 55: Stencil: Small Endless Acanthus Swirl, Royal Design Studio
Pages 58-59: Stencil: Royal Design: Woven215
Pages 60-61: Stencil: #56-1279-09; Designer Stencils; floorcloth fabric: Kunin Felt; 800-292-7900; fabric: Tulips, Calico Corners
Pages 68-69: Stencil: Plaid Floral Pavilion by Laura Ashley; fabric: Gingham Stripe (Willow); courtesy of Calico Corners
Pages 70-71: Tile Border #504, Royal Design
Pages 72-73: Fabrics: Palm Springs and Monkey Business; Calico Corners; bamboo shades: Smith+Nobles
Pages 74-75: Designer Stencils: #S1-2584-07
Pages 76-77: Courtesy of Spring 2000 Paint Décor magazine; for full-size patterns of upper and lower wall stencils, send $3.50 to Paint Décor Patterns, 1716 Locust St., GA-307, Des Moines, IA 50309-3023; ceiling medallion pattern (#CM1820): Bentley Brothers (800/824-4777); photography: Perry Struse
Page 79: Stencil: 26-2289-25, Designer Stencils
Pages 80-81: Flowers #48-2191-15; watering can#49-2028-07, Designer Stencils

U.S. UNITS TO METRIC EQUIVALENTS

To Convert From	Multiply By	To Get
Inches	25.4	Millimeters (mm)
Inches	2.54	Centimeters (cm)
Feet	30.48	Centimeters (cm)
Feet	0.3048	Meters (m)

METRIC UNITS TO U.S. EQUIVALENTS

To Convert From	Multiply By	To Get
Millimeters	0.0394	Inches
Centimeters	0.3937	Inches
Centimeters	0.0328	Feet
Meters	3.2808	Feet